Learning Practices

*Assessment and Action for
Organizational Improvement*

Dr. Anthony J. DiBella

*President, Organization Transitions, Inc.
Adjunct Professor of Management,
    Worcester Polytechnic Institute*

Prentice
Hall

Upper Saddle River, New Jersey 07458

Library of Congress Cataloging-in-Publication Data

DiBella, Anthony J., 1948-
    Learning practices : assessment and action for organizational
improvement / Anthony DiBella.
        p. cm. -- (Prentice-Hall organizational development series)
    Includes bibliographical references and index.
    ISBN 0-13-017380-0
    1. Organizational learning. I. Title. II. Series.
HD58.82 .D533 2000
658.3'124--dc21   00-039945

Executive Editor: David Shafer
Managing Editor (Editorial): Jennifer Glennon
Editorial Assistant: Kim Marsden
Assistant Editor: Michele Foresta
Media Project Manager: Michele Faranda
Executive Marketing Manager: Michael Campbell
Managing Editor (Production): Judy Leale
Production Editor: Emma Moore
Production Assistant: Keri Jean
Production Manager: Paul Smolenski
Manufacturing Buyer: Lisa Babin
Associate Director, Manufacturing: Vincent Scelta
Design Manager: Patricia Smythe
Cover Design: Jill Little
Associate Director, Multimedia Production: Karen Goldsmith
Manager, Print Production: Christina Mahon
Composition: Pre-Press Company, Inc.

This book is in the Prentice Hall Organizational Development Series.
Series Editor: Edgar H. Schein.

10 9 8 7 6 5 4 3 2
ISBN 0-13-017380-0

Series Foreword

The Prentice Hall Series on Organization Development originated in the late 1960s when a number of us recognized that the rapidly growing field of "OD" was not well understood or well defined. We also recognized that there was no one OD philosophy; hence, one could not at that time write a textbook on the theory and practice of OD, but one could make clear what various practitioners were doing under that label. So the original six books in the OD Series launched what became a continuing enterprise, the essence of which was to allow different authors to speak for themselves rather than to summarize under one umbrella what was obviously a rapidly growing and highly diverse field.

By the early 1980s, OD was growing by leaps and bounds and expanding into all kinds of organizational areas and technologies of intervention. By this time, many textbooks existed that tried to capture core concepts in the field, but we felt that diversity and innovation continued to be the more salient aspects of OD. Accordingly, our series had expanded to nineteen titles.

As we moved into the 1990s, we began to see some real convergence in the underlying assumptions of OD. As we observed how different professionals working in different kinds of organizations and occupational communities made their cases, we saw that we were still far from having a single "theory" of organizational development. Yet, some common premises were surfacing. We began to see patterns in what was working and what was not, and we were becoming more articulate about these patterns. We also started to view the field of OD as increasingly connected to other organizational sciences and disciplines, such as information technology, coordination theory, and organization theory.

In the early 90s, we added several new titles to the OD Series to describe important new themes: Ciampa's *Total Quality* illustrates the important link to employee involvement in continuous improvement; Johansen et al.'s *Leading Business Teams* explores the important arena of electronic information tools for teamwork; Tjosvold's *The Conflict-Positive Organization* shows how conflict management can turn conflict into constructive action; and Hirschhorn's *Managing in the New Team Environment* builds bridges to group psychodynamic theory.

In the mid 1990s, we continued to explore emerging themes with four revisions and three new books. Burke took his highly successful *Organization Development* into new realms with more current and expanded content; Galbraith updated and enlarged his classic theory of how information management lies at the heart of organization design with his new edition of *Competing with Flexible Lateral Organizations*; and Dyer wrote an important third edition of his classic book, *Team Building*. In addition, Rashford and Coghlan introduced the important concept of levels of organizational complexity as a basis for intervention theory in their book *The Dynamics of Organizational Levels*; in *Creating Labor-Management Partnerships*, Woodworth and Meek take us into the critical realm of how OD can help in labor relations—an area that has become increasingly important as productivity issues become critical for global competitiveness. In *Integrated Strategic Change,* authors Worley, Hitchin, and Ross powerfully demonstrate how the field of OD must be linked to the field of strategy by reviewing the role of OD at each stage of the strategy planning and implementation process. Finally, authors Argyris and Schön provided an important link to organizational learning in a new version of their classic book entitled *Organizational Learning II: Theory, Method, and Practice.*

Now, as we continue to think about the field of OD and what it will mean in the 21st century, we have added several titles that reflect the growing connections between the original concepts of OD and the wider range of the applications of these concepts. Rupert Chisholm's *Developing Network Organizations: Learning from Practice and Theory* explores and illustrates the link between OD and building community networks. In their book called *Diagnosing and Changing Organizational Culture,* Cameron and Quinn explore one model and technique of how to get at the crucial concept of culture and how to make this concept relevant for the practitioner. The theme of process consultation has remained central in OD, and we have found that it continues to be relevant in a variety of helping situations. In *Process Consultation Revisited: Building the Helping Relationship,* Schein has completely revised and updated this concept by focusing on process consultation as a general model of the helping process; his volume pulls together material from previous work and also adds new concepts and cases.

The first member of the OD series to bear a 2000 copyright is *Work-Based Learning*, by Joe Raelin. This book shows readers how to acquire learning in the midst of practice by exploring the intersection of knowledge and experience. Intended as a practical guide for a new generation of managers and executive educators, *Work-Based Learning* explores how to learn collectively with others who also wish to develop their own capability and how to engage one's reflective powers to challenge those taken-for-granted assumptions that unwittingly hold us back from questioning standard ways of operating.

The newest member of the series is *Learning Practices: Assessment and Action for Organizational Improvement* by Anthony DiBella. The primary goal of the book is to help readers recognize and use learning capability as a fact of organizational life. It provides practical details and how-tos for team and organizational learning within its Learning Orientations framework. The book guides readers in how to interpret learning profiles, select learning and knowledge management practices aligned with the values and strategic mission of their team or company, and then implement organizational learning capability plans.

Our series on Organization Development now includes over thirty titles. We will continue to welcome new titles and revisions as we explore the various frontiers of organization development and identify themes that are relevant to the ever more difficult problem of helping organizations remain effective in an increasingly turbulent environment.

New York, New York
Cambridge, Massachusetts

Richard H. Beckhard
Edgar H. Schein

As many readers may already know, my co-editor Dick Beckhard, passed away peacefully on Dec. 28, 1999 at the age of 81. We all miss his lively enthusiastic insights into the OD field and I will endeavor to keep alive a tradition that he, Warren Bennis, and I started back in 1968 with the launching of the OD series.

E. S.

Preface

Success, however you define it, is what most of us strive for. Yet success in any endeavor can produce complacency, an unwillingness to change or adapt, and the inability to learn; and that leads to failure. Whether a failure is actually a seed for growth depends on the ability to learn from experience. Changing times make organizational success fleeting and failure just one slip, miscue, or poor management decision away.

In the 21st century, successful companies will innovate and adapt, hence learn, far more quickly and effectively than their counterparts. Effective learning means shifting not only what gets learned but how learning takes place and evolves with emerging technologies; that requires linking learning and change in, of, and among organizations. This book makes those bridges.

Purpose

The aim of this book is to help readers recognize and use learning capability as a fact of organizational life. As social systems, organizations are contexts in which learning is a latent, or often hidden, form of collective action. This book indicates how learning in, of, and among organizations can be recognized, analyzed, and put into practice through a variety of learning actions and styles that improve organizational performance. Anyone involved in developing the capability of a workforce or organization to work more effectively will find value in this book.

During the past ten years the need for organizational learning and for building learning organizations has become a common call on the management scene. Many firms now invest in initiatives to acquire, create, archive, and share "best practices." While these calls have been apparent, the clarity and application of concepts and theories have lagged behind the interest of managers and practitioners to take action. Although some prescriptive approaches have been popular, there has concurrently been a realization that teams and organizations learn in a myriad of ways and that there is no one way to build a learning organization or share a "best practice." Other trends include a shift in emphasis from "training" to "learning" and the recognition that informal modes of knowledge dissemination are more critical to organizational success than formal training programs (Center for Workforce Development, 1998).

At the same time, there has been a burgeoning interest in "knowledge management," a trend that has been fairly separate from the learning organization phenomenon. While the latter has led to the creation of the CLO—Chief Learning Officer, the former has led to the creation of the CKO—Chief Knowledge Officer. There is a need to bridge the divide between these social communities with tools that link "knowledge management" with "organizational learning." Building a learning organization or creating and then using knowledge management systems are organizational innovations. Consequently, these practices can only be realized when developed within a framework of organization development (OD) or change management; an OD approach, which has been the hallmark of this book series, most clearly applies.

I regularly hear managers and practitioners articulate their interest in organizational learning and knowledge management and pose questions about how the concepts apply to their work settings or what they should do. For example, in my workshops practitioners often ask:

> "Given the demand for resources, how can I justify an investment in learning?"
>
> "What are the trade-offs and advantages of different learning approaches?"
>
> "How can we align our investments in learning with our performance measures?"
>
> "How can I help my staff learn together?"
>
> "What kind of learning organization should our company be?"
>
> "How can we best share our expertise across different parts of our company?"
>
> "Should we invest more in formal or informal learning?"
>
> "How can we learn faster?"

A major contribution of this book is to address these questions by providing the practical details and how-tos of team and organizational learning. The structure for this guidance comes from an innovative framework that includes seven different Learning Orientations (LOrs) exhibited by teams and organizations. Learning Orientations are bipolar dimensions of contrasting learning approaches, resulting in 14 (7 × 2) approaches. This book provides an inventory of learning practices that shows how capability can be developed within these 14 approaches.

Readers of this book will be guided in how to recognize and choose between alternative learning styles and methods. One way the book achieves this is by providing the *Organizational Learning Inventory* (OLI), a tool used to profile a team or organization's learning capability. This book serves as a guide for using the OLI in change interventions that improve how a team or organization creates, disseminates, or uses knowledge. It guides readers in how to interpret their learning profiles and select learning and knowledge management practices that are aligned with the values and strategic mission of their team or company.

While the OLI should be used in what traditionally has been an essential element of OD, diagnosis, that first step is simply that—a first step—followed by strategic action. Plans to build organizational learning capability are bound to fail where there is a deficit in implementation. Consequently, this book also addresses critical issues in implementation, such as how to adapt learning methods and styles to different contexts and how to promote staff identification and commitment to borrowed "best practices."

Some History

This book is based on: (1) extensive knowledge of the literature about what learning organizations are and how they can be created and about change management, (2) in-depth research in seven American and European companies that focused on understanding how and why organizations learn, and (3) field experience in testing materials and developing learning practices with executive managers, operations staff, and human resource and organization development consultants and managers in over 100 Global 1000 companies.

In 1992, the author, along with two MIT colleagues, Edwin Nevis and Janet Gould, began a research program entitled "Organizations as Learning Systems." (Over the course of four years, the program received funding from the Healthcare Forum and the International Consortium for Executive Development Research, and administrative support from the Center for Organizational Learning at MIT.) Among the companies involved in the testing and development stage were AT&T, British Petroleum, Burroughs Wellcome, EDS, Exxon Chemical, Heineken, Merck, PacBell, and Unilever. This program evolved through different stages to include grounded fieldwork, action learning and action research workshops, designing and testing a train-the-trainers program, publications in professional journals, and speaking and consulting engagements with a variety of business and not-for-profit organizations.

During the past five years the ideas and materials from this program have been incorporated into a training program entitled "Building Organizational Learning Capability," for which a *Strategies Workbook* and a *Facilitator's Guide* have been written. In workshops and client engagements, this program has been used with staff from a diverse set of companies such as Boeing, Chase Manhattan Bank, Children's Hospital–San Diego, Eastman Kodak, Hewlett-Packard, Motorola, Nortel Networks, Northwest Airlines, Oracle, Shell, and Telecom Italia. Presently, I conduct public workshops to use the program, even as we continue research to monitor its applications, adapt it to different industries, and study the outcomes of different learning methods.

Outline

Part I establishes the reasons for investing in learning capability and lays out the steps to assessment and diagnosis. Chapter 1 discusses the need for learning within the context of what we know about organizational change, corporate strategy, and methods for intervention and diagnosis. After Chapter 1, the book is designed to get readers immediately into the task of assessment. The cornerstone of this process is using the *Organizational Learning Inventory* (OLI) as a tool for any organizational unit, such as a department, workgroup, task force, or a company subsidiary, to profile its learning capability and align it with the strategic direction of a team or company.

The OLI is designed to generate dialogue among group members who share their knowledge and perceptions about the group's learning and thereby create their own learning profile. The learning profile gives the group a starting point to understand its current learning capability, but the generation of the profile is itself an intervention and a process of group learning. In Chapters 2 and 3 readers work through the assessment process and develop their baseline learning profile. Then Chapter 4 considers how to recognize an organization's best or desired profile.

Part II of this book focuses on prescriptions to build that desired profile. Learning practices and other interventions are considered within the context of the assessment done in Part I. Consequently, the tone of Chapters 5 and 6 is more directive than suggestive. Chapter 7 takes readers out beyond the boundaries of their own teams or organizations to examine the challenges of learning across those boundaries. For example, sharing "best practices" has become a popular tactic for organizational improvement in many companies. Yet lessons of experience are not easily transferred. What can managers do about that? This question is the focus of Chapter 7.

As indicated by the table of contents, the book builds up from the assessment process (Part I) of a particular team or organization into more strategic and long-term learning issues. Consequently, the final section of the book, Part III, is directed to readers who want to reach further to maximize the return on their learning investments. Chapter 8 considers how the learning practices within companies form patterns and portfolios that need to be managed strategically. Chapter 9 examines several critical challenges facing companies that try to learn. This chapter reviews the concept of "best practices," which are treated not as unchangeable universals but as ideas or techniques that are subject to interpretation and adaptation. The final chapter looks at how the dimensions of space and time relate to our learning and can be circumvented through innovative means.

Acknowledgments

Foremost, I want to acknowledge Ed Nevis for bringing me into his research while we were both at MIT. We collaborated on the early phases of research that serve as anchors for this book and produced several joint publications. Somehow, as our careers and life paths diverged, I came to extend the trail that he, along with Janet Gould, started and that for five years we built and trod together. Ed is now enjoying retirement from MIT but is still active in the Gestalt Institute of Cleveland, which he cofounded. I also want to thank Janet Gould, who contributed to the *Strategies Workbook* from which some of the material in this book was adapted. Doug Ready and the International Consortium for Executive Development Research were important early financial sponsors of our research.

Another major contributor to my work and thinking has been Ed Schein, not merely for supporting this book as part of the OD series, but for his own intellectual and practical achievements, which have been a well-spring of insight and inspiration. It comes as no surprise to me that there are far more references to Ed's work in this book than to anyone else's. Another Ed, Ed Deevy, read an early version of my manuscript and made several valuable comments that I have incorporated in the final draft.

Others sources of intellectual and emotional support and encouragement over the years include Marjorie Ball, Mac Banks, Michael Brower, Steve Cabana, Melissa Cefkin, Michael Courtney, Nikki and Stephen Downes-Martin, Ted Kahn, Jeff Kelley, Joe Raelin, Kim Slack, John Van Maanen, Helen Vassallo, the Rhode Island Writer's Circle, and the Greater Boston ODN book group. Finally, I would like to thank David Shafer at Prentice Hall for his guidance and support and his colleagues, Emma Moore and Kim Marsden, for their help with production.

Follow-up and Feedback

Book writing and book reading are separate and solitary activities; and traditionally, book authors and book buyers have been isolated from one another. For most readers, authors merely represent names on cover pages, book covers, and spines. Authors rarely get to know who is buying their books. Modern forms of communication provide a means to bridge this separation.

Although I cannot be with you as you read this, please know that I am accessible through that most modern form of communication, the Internet. If you have any questions about the ideas, methods, or learning practices described in this book, please contact me via e-mail at "ajdibella@orgtransitions.com." As prompted, I will answer your questions or offer clarifications.

I am also very interested in your reaction to this book and your own experiences in promoting learning practices in teams and organizations. For that reason, I have created space on the World Wide Web to post your insight on topics covered in this book. Just log onto the Web and direct your browser to *www.orgtransitions.com*. There you will find a means to submit your post for other site visitors to read. In this way our mutual learning experience can be enhanced and maintained beyond the traditional constraints of time, space, and the printed page.

I wish you a rewarding life's journey, enriched through learning.

Tony DiBella
East Greenwich, Rhode Island, USA,
Planet Earth, Milky Way

*To my parents, Rosario (Sam) DiBella and Mary DiCarlo DiBella,
who made the investment (and sacrifice) to promote my learning.*

Contents

Preface

Part I

Profiles of Learning: Current and Strategic

Assessment and diagnosis are traditional first steps in OD interventions. The chapters in Part I establish the basis for a learning approach to work settings and provide an assessment tool to profile learning capability. The challenge of modifying learning approaches for strategic alignment and competitive advantage is presented.

1

The Competitive Edge: Learning for Strategic Advantage

Learning is not compulsory but neither is survival.
—W. Edwards Deming

The Call to Learn

Support for education and learning is a controversial topic in modern society. On the one hand, the economic, technological, and social development experienced during the past few centuries could not have occurred without substantial backing for various forms of formal and informal learning. In many cases that learning resulted from the pursuit of science, which is a formal and structured learning method. Yet critics complain that this pursuit has come at some cost (deterioration of our physical environment and ecosystem, increasing violence and anomie, greater work demands), which has produced a zealous reaction in some parts of our world for a return to so-called traditional values.

Meanwhile, with a growing perception of declining resources amidst greater demands, investment decisions are increasingly made on the basis of immediate or short-term gains. Reflective of this trend is the relative decline in liberal arts education, since it is not vocation directed, and student dislike for case-based course requirements (just in case you can use it). Yet successful, or as Collins and Porras (1994) would say, "visionary companies" are those that have come to recognize that you cannot predict the outcome and ultimate value of educational investments. Success in the marketplace requires efficiency of current operations combined with the foresight or preparedness to either be an innovator or adapt to the innovations of others. The former comes from learning through continuous improvement processes, the latter from a belief that investments in learning lead to innovation in unpredictable and unforeseen ways and that those who fail to adapt are preparing to fail.

While the need to justify the gains from any investment contrasts with the recognition that learning has an important but uncertain payoff, there has been a growing appreciation and felt need for learning, whether in or of organizations. During the past 10 years, interest in organizational learning and knowledge management has grown at a seemingly exponential rate following the publication of Peter Senge's book, *The Fifth Discipline* (1990) and five books with the same title, *Intellectual Capital* (Hudson, 1993; Brooking, 1996; Edvinsson & Malone, 1997; Stewart, 1997; Roos, 1998). In fact, the roots of current practitioner interest go back to the quality movement and its focus on continuous improvement, hence learning and knowledge creation, and before that to the notion that organizations comprise systems of decision making or information processing (March & Simon, 1958; Cyert & March, 1963). Whether it was due to the emergence of a global economy or an increase in competitiveness among firms, learning has become a strategic initiative for many organizations (deGeus, 1988) and a focal point for competitive advantage (Stata, 1989).

Most of this literature, developed in the past ten years, that considers organizational learning or the learning organization follows a normative or prescriptive tradition. That is, specific conditions must be in place for learning to occur and to offset the barriers and learning disabilities that organizations traditionally suffer (Snyder & Cummings, 1992). The basic difference between authors is in the elements or conditions that comprise the prescription. For example, David Garvin (1993), Michael McGill (1992), and Peter Senge (1990) each list a mix of behaviors, skills, or conditions including systems thinking, team learning, creativity, and experimentation, that must be in place for learning to occur. These authors presume that organizations have properties dysfunctional to learning and that the key to building learning capability is to overcome these constraints by supporting an environment that is conducive to learning.

This book is based on a different set of assumptions about organizations, assumptions that are consistent with traditional principles of organization development, or OD. They include the presumption that all social systems have worthwhile characteristics and that the seeds of an organization's development and ultimate success lie within itself. The challenge is to recognize (through such techniques as appreciative inquiry) inherent value and to develop shared mechanisms (such as dialogue) whereby strategic, productive development can occur.

Learning Masquerades

While "learning" per se as a topic of management focus has come into vogue, learning activities have been characteristic of successful organizations for many years. They simply have come under different names, labels, or types of intervention. Consider the following managerial activities or organizational domains:

Innovation

Research (Ries & Trout, 1981) has shown that being first to market with a new product or service provides a company with a distinctive competitive advantage. To do so requires innovation or corporate creativity (Robinson & Stern, 1998), which is a form of learning. Innovation is about learning new ways to understand or configure the world around us. It is about seeing possibilities while others see constraints, converting failure into success, or acting in novel ways. Innovation pertains to creating new knowledge or using existing knowledge in ways that create new forms of thinking or new products. In that sense the results of innovation are transformative since the outcome is something entirely different from what you had before.

One result may be new product markets or categories that allow organizations to successfully compete for the future (Hamel & Prahalad, 1994). It should not be surprising that at 3M, a company renowned for innovation, staff are discouraged from killing new product ideas and encouraged to tolerate honest mistakes (Collins & Porras, 1994). It is no doubt this orientation that led staff to recognize the benefits of a poorly performing adhesive and to use that knowledge to create a series of Post-It Notes products.

Continuous Improvement

The Japanese management practice of Quality Circles evolved in the 1960s and 1970s into the Total Quality Management movement (TQM) in the 1980s. A basic element of TQM is the use of feedback and measurement systems and processes to increase performance (Deming, 1982; Juran, 1992). Whether you label this process single-loop learning (Argyris, 1976) or *kaizen* (Imai, 1989), it's all about learning to get better and better at what you already do through many small incremental improvements. This type of learning occurs through the close and continuous monitoring and analysis of one's own work processes.

Fidelity Investments is one of the world's largest and most successful financial services firms. Perhaps it's no wonder then that its CEO, Ned Johnson, is a strong advocate of *kaizen*. One result at Fidelity is the continuous development of new support systems for back-office operations. Such administrative domains constitute much of the often hidden work of financial services firms and provide a potential source for increasing efficiencies.

Continuous Adaptation

Learning how to improve performance based on one's own experience is strictly an internal matter. Competitive advantage also derives from learning to respond to shifts in a company's external environment. The latter may pertain to changes in customer needs or wants, a competitor's strategy, or the introduction of new technology. Firms must continually adapt to changes in market conditions or else be subject to such ignominious disabilities as marketing myopia and the not-invented-here syndrome. It is often said of championship athletic teams that "they find a way to win." This testament refers to the capability of a team to adjust to the circumstances of any game and to react in such a way (to either change their game plan, their plays, players, or tactics) to ensure victory.

The business literature contains examples of many well-known companies (such as Motorola, who went from making car radios to learning how to manufacture and market computer chips and cell phones) that have found a way to evolve and adapt to market conditions. Another intriguing but lesser-known example is Hasbro, the world's second-largest toy maker. Merrill Hassenfeld, father of Hasbro's current CEO, started in business by buying scrap fabrics and materials from the cutting rooms of garment manufacturers and using them to make cleaning rags. He then learned that fabric was a good stuffing material and used what he had to make stuffed animals. This led his company into the toy market (G.I. Joe, Mr. Potato Head) and from there to board games and now interactive games on compact discs.

Benchmarking

If you combine an emphasis on innovation and continuous improvement with adapting to the external environment, you end up with a powerful combination. For this reason many companies have sought to learn not only from their own experiences but also from the experiences of others, including their competitors. One way to do so has become known as "benchmarking," measuring someone else's performance against your own. Comparing the performance of two similar or apparently identical organizations is an important learning activity. The outcome may confirm or disconfirm how well company staff think they are doing, but the key of benchmarking is having a relative point of comparison. For example, the most successful competitors for the America's Cup sailing trophy are those syndicates that have at least two boats with which to train and practice. By match racing boats of similar design, skippers can learn about the relative benefits of different equipment or racing tactics. As one boat gains an advantage, the other boat must compensate by learning ways to increase boat speed or improve crew performance.

Benchmarking takes time, so it is best done when an organization is not in crisis but has slack resources (such as money or time) that can be devoted to learning. In 1989 Fiat Automobile had one of its most successful years. In the same year its CEO authorized studies to benchmark Fiat's performance against that of other automobile makers and manufacturers of large consumer goods. The benchmarking was done by having 50 of Fiat's top managers visit manufacturing plants worldwide. Through this exercise Fiat came to learn (from Chrysler) about simultaneous engineering and (from Ford) about total quality planning.

Learning Defined

The four activities briefly described in the preceding paragraphs have a common thread—their aim is to "maintain or improve team or organizational performance based on experience"—and that is the essence of learning. Performance of a group, team, organization, or corporation can be improved for many reasons, including changes in the market environment, serendipity, or chance. For example, performance (as measured by increased sales or net revenue) can improve because a competitor went out of business or due to higher consumer confidence. In changing environments, companies need to learn just to maintain the same relative performance.

Whether reacting to circumstances around them or proactively looking for ways to get better, learning is not an accidental event. It takes resources—whether time, money, skill, or just a certain mental attitude. Even serendipitous learning, which occurs due to some unexpected event, requires that we be open and ready to recognize and take advantage of circumstances as they present themselves. Events occur (whether Newton being hit by an apple, the overflow of Archimedes's bathtub, or Hasbro's access to rags) that can lead us to learn and with that learning make us more effective in the world around us.

Learning Models: Cases from Industry, Organization, and Workgroup Levels

While learning can be serendipitous, it can also be transparent. When we learn in small increments, we often fail to realize it's happening or how much we have learned over time. Learning becomes such an ongoing process that we don't see it when it occurs. This characteristic can best be seen on an industry level when operations represent the aggregate learning of many different organizations.

Take, for example, the airline industry, which each day moves over one million passengers in the United States and millions more worldwide. These numbers represent an incredible increase in the scale of activity from when the Wright brothers powered the first aircraft at the beginning of the 20th century. More impressive than the scale of operations is the relative increase in safety. Since civil aviation became an industry, the number of accidents resulting in injury has decreased during each succeeding decade.

A principal reason for this change is that the aviation industry has learned how to operate more aircraft more safely over time. A major contribution to this progression is that every aircraft accident is treated as a learning opportunity. Whenever there is a crash of a civilian airplane, public or private, the National Transportation Safety Board (NTSB) opens a formal panel of inquiry as to why that accident occurred and what should be done to prevent similar occurrences. Participating on such panels are representatives from airline companies, airplane manufacturers, trade unions, manufacturers of aircraft parts, public officials, and consumers. The results of a panel's work may lead to the redesign of a plane or its components, revised maintenance procedures, new forms of training, or new procedures to coordinate the work between pilots and air traffic controllers. Each lesson learned, when applied properly, leads to a bigger and safer industry.

The success of NTSB's learning experience parallels the initiatives in industries to create learning communities or collaborations. For example, following the nuclear accident at Three Mile Island, Pennsylvania, in 1979 the nuclear power industry established its Institute for Nuclear Power Operations. Now nuclear power operators have institutional mechanisms to share their lessons from experience and ensure a safer industry.

These and other industry examples provide a context for learning that is often hidden from the consumer. The ubiquity and effusiveness of learning also occurs on a company or organizational level. Motorola is often cited in the business literature for its ability to learn and adapt. Beginning as a manufacturer of battery eliminators, Motorola has transformed itself, through the development of different product lines, to respond to changing market conditions and technologies. As overt as these changes have been, Motorola has also spawned an entire movement for firms to learn incrementally and covertly through continuous improvement processes.

When Motorola learned in the 1970s that its manufacturing quality was inferior to that of its Japanese competitors, it developed an approach to continuous improvement called "Six Sigma." That program establishes ongoing processes to learn from customers, competitors, and employees. Motorola's "Six Sigma" program has become well known; positive results have led to its adoption by other companies such as Du Pont, General Electric, and Raytheon.

In changing times, learning also occurs surreptitiously at the group or workteam level. A good place to see it is in the field of medical services. Ongoing changes in medical technology, instrumentation, and medication require doctors and nurses to constantly update or expand their set of skills. From transplant to bypass surgery to angioplasty, CAT scans to MRIs, one cancer treatment protocol to another, medical practitioners constantly learn about innovative products and methods.

This learning process is so ongoing that it's reflected in a saying familiar to medical practitioners—"See one, do one, teach one." The need for learning occurs so often and so rapidly and unexpectedly that there's no time for formal, in-class training programs. In a quest for better health for their patients, practitioners learn from one another on the job and on the go through osmosis, observation, and role modeling.

Learning as Collective or Social Action

The preceding cases each reflect the social nature of learning. Through the coordinated inquiries and reflections of a set of people and stakeholders, any experience can be converted into a learning opportunity. Investments in research can also be made to proactively seek answers to questions that unlock the doors of innovation. Whether the learning takes place from looking at the past (what has already happened) or the future (what might happen), most forms of learning are inherently social since they involve action among a set of individuals.

Learning, however, is social not just because it involves coordinated action, but because it is a required process in any system wherein individuals interact. A distinctive feature of our species is the need to create cultures and learn how to function within them. Culture is a shared set of assumptions, values, and artifacts (Schein, 1992). Over time mechanisms get created to process collective experience and share it with new members. The result is an embedded set of learning methods. Some advocates of learning in organizations have urged the creation of so-called "learning cultures," but this call represents an improper or antiquated view of cultures since it presumes that learning is a characteristic of some rather than all living systems. Various studies done at the Institute for Research on Learning have shown that learning, whether through formal or informal mechanisms, is a fundamental part of social life (Lave & Wenger, 1991). Any approach to building learning capability in teams or organizations must be based on this fundamental characteristic.

From Training to Learning

One result from increased competition in today's marketplace and various efforts at promoting organizational efficiency, such as business process engineering, has been the reduction in discretionary time in the workforce. Employees have less time for activities that are not viewed as immediately productive. Since classroom training takes an employee away from present responsibilities, supervisors and senior managers have become less supportive of training activities, which has contributed to a popular shift in focus from training to learning.

Training has also lost some appeal because of rapidly changing circumstances in the workplace. The content of formal training programs can lose relevance by the time it's actually presented in the classroom. While training may be a one-time affair, learning is ongoing.

An orientation toward training emphasizes the need to know or use what someone else has learned, whereas with learning, the responsibility for content shifts from the trainer to the learner. Greater reliance is placed on learning through improvisation rather than through didactic experiences. Besides increasing the relevance of what gets learned, the learner more readily identifies with it. The new challenge is how to get learners to identify with the knowledge and insight generated by others without their having to reinvent the wheel.

Learning Overload and Smart Learning

Placing the responsibility for learning in the workforce on the individual makes sense when we are referring to individual capabilities. Yet as Chris Argyris (1957) discussed many years ago, individual versus organizational needs and interests are apt to be incongruent. Whether an individual's learning initiatives are aligned with an organization's interest cannot be presumed. The potential for this nonalignment of learning interests is intensified when we factor in the notion that knowledge is infinite and it's getting bigger all the time. The desire to keep up with one's profession can propel an individual to learn indiscriminately. In the information age, individuals face learning overload and learning all sorts of things that have little value within the context of their work environment. Consequently, the issue of relevant learning is a critical one.

Learning does have intrinsic value, and one can never say or know how something learned today may help someone or some group at a subsequent time. The key to effective learning is coming to know what you need to know when you need it. Strategic learning means selectively processing information. Learning smart in the information age involves strategically figuring out what you need to know and then taking action to acquire that knowledge.

As much as individuals and organizations should be aware of what they know, and what they need to learn, they must also be cognizant of those processes whereby learning takes place. Understanding how you learn is as much a part of a strategic approach as knowing whether what you know is what you need to know. Individuals and organizations can selectively choose learning modes that fit their style, the nature of their learning, and their team or organization culture. The selection of a learning method is dependent on learning content, timeframe, resources, and processing modes.

So while learning is a necessary attribute for any team and organization to be successful, indiscriminate learning will be more of a drain on resources than a source of competitive advantage. To recognize that learning is a critical capability in a fast-moving business environment (and that's the context in which businesses must operate) makes for good theory since it encourages an allocation of resources to learning. What is unanswered is how strategic learning capabilities are going to be developed. At this juncture the nature and relevance of OD provides the answer.

OD Steps to Build Learning Capability

Promoting and building learning capability in organizations means promoting change. OD practitioners have traditionally followed certain values or precepts when considering any form of intervention. For example, OD as a profession values the abilities and sensibilities of individual workers and their workteams to understand and solve their own problems; the role of the OD consultant is to promote, not dictate, such processes.

To build organizational learning capability with an OD approach requires three main steps (See Figure 1-1):

1. Recognize and Appreciate Existing Learning
2. Establish a Gap Between Existing Learning and Strategic Learning Needs
3. Identify Actions to Build Desired Learning Capability

Step 1. Recognize and Appreciate Existing Learning

To claim that organizational learning has occurred means that new knowledge has come into a social system and has been disseminated and used (DiBella & Nevis, 1998). Organizational learning requires all three processes in this cycle. Unless knowledge is shared, it remains the property of individuals rather than the organization at large. As property of the organization, it is accessible and applied at some level, since at a minimum new knowledge changes one's capacity to act.

Figure 1-1
OD Approach to Build Organizational Learning Capability

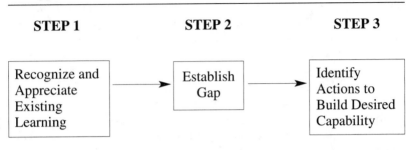

An OD approach to building learning capability needs to describe existent learning processes in organizations without being prescriptive. Research has generated a method for doing so. While Shrivastava (1983) was the first to describe different styles of organizational learning, subsequent research has led to a more complete framework. Nevis, DiBella, and Gould (1995) identified seven distinctive learning processes, which they labeled Learning Orientations (LOrs). LOrs reflect practices by which knowledge is acquired, disseminated, or used. They are descriptive elements represented as paired contrasts situated along a continuum for which there is no right or wrong location. Every organization has a distinctive position along each continuum, and these positions in aggregate constitute an organization's learning style.

While learning is an embedded process in any social system, research has revealed that learning can be promoted and guided when certain conditions or Facilitating Factors (FFs) are in place (DiBella & Nevis, 1998). Thus, to understand learning capability requires an examination of both descriptive and normative factors. The former are represented by LOrs—how learning takes place—while the latter reflect FFs—how well a team works its style and uses it in a strategic manner. DiBella and Nevis (1998) identified 10 Facilitating Factors that when combined with the seven LOrs constitute an organization's learning profile.

To focus a group's attention requires a clear framework to recognize common concerns and build consensus. A visual tool can help team members understand strategic learning needs and priorities. Such a mechanism can promote a shared vision about learning approaches and indicate a direction for change. Figure 1-2 contains the format for the "Organizational Learning Profile" that serves these purposes.

The learning profile depicts each LOr as a continuum of approaches and is a convenient way to focus a group and to represent its own data. Working together, members of an organization can dialogue about what learning processes are used by their team or firm. Their focal point should be the different learning approaches represented by the seven LOr continuums. For example, groups can reflect on how or if they use knowledge from their own experience (*internal Knowledge Source*) or from the experiences of others (*external Knowledge Source*). Are they apt to learn about existing products or methods (*incremental Learning Scope*) or entirely new ones (*transformative Learning Scope*)? Team members can depict their learning approaches as being toward one end or the other of each continuum. Where the emphasis is balanced, a mid-point location would be appropriate. Since FFs are normative, they are presented on a numerical or point scale.

Step 2. Establish a Gap Between Existing Learning and Strategic Learning Needs

To acknowledge and appreciate existing learning capabilities is ennobling and empowering but not sufficient to motivate change. Creating a gap between current and desired learning capability provides a basis for action. Once groups have depicted their learning approaches, they need to consider whether those approaches serve their strategic needs. In other words, although the organization is learning, to what extent does the content of that learning meet the performance pressures and environmental demands of the organization? Such a consideration is consistent with the principles of OD since at a minimum it recognizes and builds on what already exists. Also the choice about shifting orientations or strengthening FFs is based on knowledge within the team or organization rather than on the basis of a consultant's prescriptions. Building desired learning capability means aligning what a team or organization learns with its performance demands or strategy. Through the use of symbols (A, B), current (A) and desired (B) learning capabilities can be represented on an "Organizational Learning Profile."

By surfacing existing, although perhaps transparent, capabilities, an OD approach empowers individuals to acknowledge the

Figure 1-2
Organizational Learning Profile, Example

LEARNING ORIENTATIONS:

		Mostly	More	Even	More	Mostly	
1. Knowledge Source	Internal		A	B			External
2. Content–Process Focus	Content	B			A		Process
3. Knowledge Reserve	Personal		A	B			Public
4. Dissemination Mode	Formal		A		B		Informal
5. Learning Scope	Incremental		A	B			Trans-formative
6. Value–Chain Focus	Design-Make	B			A		Market-Deliver
7. Learning Focus	Individual		A	B			Group

	Little Evidence to Support This Factor		Some Evidence to Support This Factor			Extensive Evidence to Support This Factor	
FACILITATING FACTORS:	1	2	3	4	5	6	7
1. Scanning Imperative		A		B			
2. Performance Gap			A		B		
3. Concern for Measurement				B			A
4. Organizational Curiosity						AB	
5. Climate of Openness			A			B	
6. Continuous Education				A		B	
7. Operational Variety			AB				
8. Multiple Advocates					A	B	
9. Involved Leadership			AB				
10. Systems Perspective				A			B

A= current capability
B= desired capability

present and to use that awareness as a takeoff point for desired competencies. As Rouse (1996) points out, there is no better place to begin an intervention than by focusing on the capability existing in the here and now. Preparing a learning profile is an intervention to uncover existing capabilities in organizations and to affirm rather than critique experience. This approach builds on the notion that recognition of what has been accomplished is validating and energizing for those involved and is consistent with appreciative inquiry, a consulting approach advocated by some change agents (Srivastva & Cooperrider, 1999).

Step 3. Identify Actions to Build
Desired Learning Capability

In the process of developing their profile of existing capabilities, groups inevitably discuss how that profile differs from what it may have been in the past, what they think it should be, and whether it may be shifting. This shared insight provides a starting point for groups to conduct action planning on ways to build learning capability. Once the gap between current (A) and desired (B) learning capability has been established, a group can identify initiatives that focus on strategic learning issues.

The key is to let the group's own knowledge about the potentialities and leverage points for change guide the action planning process. Instead of imposing a solution for developing learning capability, a facilitator would prompt a group to come up with its own problem definition (as reflected in the gap between the current and desired profiles [A vs. B]) and solution (action plans). In this way, the outcome is a set of interventions that has group ownership and builds upon a group's own knowledge.

The data generated for points "A" on the learning profile can be used to monitor a group's progress in building learning capability. In effect, the data at "A" represent a benchmark or starting point prior to any change interventions. After a company or team has taken action, it can assess its progress by recreating new data points and seeing how they compare with the initial benchmarks.

The Role of the OD Consultant

Given the availability of popular normative models of the learning organization, consultants, whether internal or external, may find it easy to follow such prescriptions. OD consultants need to recognize that underlying any prescription is a set of theories pertaining to what organizations are and how learning and change occur. Rather than direct a client organization that wants to become a learning organization toward discrete conditions or practices, an OD consultant works with a client to first uncover existent learning capabilities and treats such an assessment as an intervention (Schein, 1999a). The focus is to promote client awareness of what is and how that capability can be enhanced and aligned with strategic learning requirements.

Frameworks like the "Organizational Learning Profile" promote such awareness. Clients can use the data portrayed on a learning profile to build their own understanding of what it would mean to be a learning organization. Ultimately, it is the shared meaning given to a concept that makes it a powerful mechanism for change.

Using the *Organizational Learning Inventory*

The "Organizational Learning Profile" is a template designed to reflect a team's or an organization's learning capability. The presentation of such data is itself an intervention since it changes how individual members view their teams or organizations. How such data are generated is also an intervention since it represents the outcome of some process to create shared meaning. A traditional way to do this in action research is through the use of diagnostic instruments. The process whereby instruments are used and their results interpreted provides an opportunity for a consultant to engage a team or organization in meaningful reflection.

Chapters 2 and 3 of this book contain the two major sections of the *Organizational Learning Inventory,* or OLI. The OLI is an instrument that guides a team in how to create its learning profile. The first section (Chapter 2) covers the seven Learning Orientations that collectively represent learning style. The second section (Chapter 3) covers the Facilitating Factors.

The OLI was designed as an interactive process to profile both the current and desired learning capability of an organizational unit, such as a department, workgroup, task force, or company subsidiary. To serve as an intervention and vehicle for dialogue, the OLI is not a self-administered questionnaire whose results are computer analyzed and then returned anonymously to the unit being profiled, nor is it expert scored. Instead, the OLI is designed as a participatory group exercise, completed by members of an organization working together with minimal assistance or direction from a trained facilitator.

Its format stimulates group discussion, providing an opportunity for group members to share knowledge and perceptions about their own learning practices. Through consensus, groups generate their learning profile and recognize unique resources and capabilities. In completing their profile of existing capabilities, groups inevitably come to reflect on what that profile should be. Once a gap has been established between current and desired learning capability, the group can identify training needs that focus on learning issues.

Learning Practices: Lesson 1

Learning is an embedded, multifaceted process in all social systems. There are many ways to improve performance. We first need to acknowledge existent learning practices before we can enhance them or successfully add new ones.

2

Assessing Learning in Your Team or Company: Learning Orientations

I am not discouraged, because every wrong attempt discarded is another step forward.

—Thomas Edison

Organizational Learning Inventory, Part 1

This chapter leads you to the first step in building organizational learning capability—assessment using the *Organizational Learning Inventory* (OLI). The OLI was developed from research, tested in various work and industry settings, and then subsequently refined. It is designed to assess a workgroup or organizational unit as a learning system. Through a process of open discussion or individual decision making, data points are generated that, in aggregate, form a learning profile. The entire learning profile can be analyzed in terms of learning style, learning strengths and weaknesses, and strategic alignment.

The business unit that is assessed may be of almost any size or focus—a functional department, a cross-functional team, a matrixed project task force, an operational workgroup, or a division or subsidiary of a larger company. The OLI may also be used to profile an entire firm or institution. The key is to assess the learning capability of some social or collective unit, as opposed to the learning of a particular individual. (For assessment of individual learning styles, see Kolb [1974] or Honey [1986].)

The version of the OLI contained in this chapter and Chapter 3 has been designed for you, the individual reader, to complete. The results of this assessment could be used in various ways. For example, the results may lead you to rethink the role of various company or team activities in contributing to learning or simply to revise your own training investments. A more engaging use of the assessment would be to compare the data you generate with how your colleagues would assess the same unit. Similarities and differences of opinion among members of a team are fruitful starting points for the development of shared action plans to improve the strategic alignment of learning capability. In fact, the OLI was initially designed as a dialogue tool to promote conversations and group awareness about a team's learning capability.

Part 1 of the OLI, as contained in this chapter, asks you to assess your team's Learning Orientations (LOr)—the practices that reflect how and where learning takes place and the nature of what is learned. There are seven Orientations or dimensions, as derived from research (DiBella, 1996), that define learning style. Table 2-1 contains a list of the seven LOrs and their definitions. Figure 2-1 is a template to capture this portion of your team's learning profile. By completing this part of the OLI, you generate seven data points that are descriptive in nature. By themselves they do not tell us whether the learning style is right or wrong, too little or too much. That sort of evaluation comes later (in Chapter 4) when we analyze or interpret this picture and determine whether it can or should be improved.

Selecting a Unit to Profile

The first step in completing the OLI is to decide what organizational unit will be the subject or focus of the profile you create. Ideally, it should be a social unit of which you are a member and that you know well. The more intimately you know the group, the easier and more valid your results will be. The OLI is best used to profile the learning capability of an established organizational unit but may also be used with new groups to facilitate their formation.

Statement Pairs

Each of the seven LOrs is presented on a separate page in this chapter. For each LOr, a definition is provided followed by a pair of statements that reflect the continuum of positions or approaches concerning the Orientation. Reading the paired statements helps you determine your

Table 2-1
Learning Orientations

1. Knowledge Source	Preference for developing knowledge internally as compared to preference for acquiring knowledge developed externally
2. Content–Process Focus	Emphasis on knowledge about **what** products or services are as compared to emphasis on knowledge about **how** those products or services are developed, or delivered, or improved
3. Knowledge Reserve	Knowledge is possessed by individuals as compared to knowledge that is publicly available
4. Dissemination Mode	Knowledge is shared in formal, prescribed methods as compared to knowledge that is shared through informal methods, such as role-modeling and casual interaction
5. Learning Scope	Preference for knowledge related to the improvement of existing products, services, or capabilities as compared to preference for knowledge related to the development of new ones
6. Value–Chain Focus	Emphasis on learning investments in engineering or production activities ("design and make" functions) versus sales or service ("market and deliver" functions)
7. Learning Focus	Development of knowledge and skills pertaining to individual performance as compared to the development of knowledge and skills pertaining to group performance

group's position along each continuum. The paired statements are designed to aid you in reflecting on the nature of your group's learning activities and in developing a greater comprehension of its Learning Orientations. After reading each pair, check the box corresponding to the statement that best describes your unit.

The OLI was designed for use in various industries and settings. Consequently, not all paired items will be relevant or even comprehensible to everyone using the OLI. If this should occur, just skip the item or think about how it might apply to your team.

Overall Rating: Profiling Your Group or Organization

At the bottom of each page, a five-step scale provides a space for you to mark your group's learning approach on each LOr. Each Orientation's two polar approaches are listed at opposite ends of the scale, and a mark at one end ("mostly") indicates that your group puts a great deal of emphasis on that learning approach. A mark toward the middle of the scale ("more," "even") means that your group uses both learning approaches to some extent or to an equal extent.

By reflecting on the meaning of the paired statements and making decisions on each one, you should come to understand your group's relative position on each continuum. The more paired statements you select representing a particular approach, the more your group's profile should be down that end of the LOr continuum. Mark an "X" in the box that best represents the orientation of the workgroup or unit you are profiling.

Summary Profile

After completing each LOr, copy your assessment or data points onto the learning profile template (Figure 2-1) located below.

Figure 2-1
Template for Learning Orientations

LEARNING ORIENTATIONS:

		Mostly	More	Even	More	Mostly	
1. Knowledge Source	Internal						External
2. Content–Process Focus	Content						Process
3. Knowledge Reserve	Personal						Public
4. Dissemination Mode	Formal						Informal
5. Learning Scope	Incremental						Trans-formative
6. Value–Chain Focus	Design-Make						Market-Deliver
7. Learning Focus	Individual						Group

Learning Orientation 1
Knowledge Source

Definition
Preference for developing knowledge internally as compared to preference for acquiring knowledge developed externally

Directions
For each pair, check the box that best describes your workgroup or organization.

	Internal	**External**
Pair 1	☐ We value the knowledge we gain from our own experience.	☐ We value the knowledge created by others.
Pair 2	☐ We encourage learning from our own actions and are likely to be an innovator in the way we do things.	☐ We encourage learning from the actions of others and are likely to emulate the work of others.
Pair 3	☐ We believe in being the first to develop a new product or technique.	☐ We believe in improving on the work of others.
Pair 4	☐ We develop new products or services ourselves.	☐ We develop new products or services in collaboration with others.
Pair 5	☐ We measure performance based on our own knowledge.	☐ We measure performance using data from the external environment.

Overall Rating
Using your above responses as a guide, mark an "X" in the box that best represents your workgroup or organization:

INTERNAL	Mostly	More	Even	More	Mostly	EXTERNAL

Learning Orientation 2
Content–Process Focus

Definition
Emphasis on knowledge about **what** products or services are as compared to emphasis on knowledge about **how** those products or services are developed, delivered, or improved

Directions
For each pair, check the box that best describes your workgroup or organization.

	Content	**Process**
Pair 1	☐ We invest in research and development on what our products or services should be.	☐ We invest in research and development on how to create or deliver our products or services.
Pair 2	☐ We are likely to acquire knowledge from others about the content of their products.	☐ We are likely to acquire knowledge from others about how they assemble, market, or deliver their products.
Pair 3	☐ Individuals who create or deliver our products are appreciated more than those who support them.	☐ Individuals who support operational teams are appreciated as much or more than those who create or deliver our products.
Pair 4	☐ We regard process expenses as overhead required to create and deliver our products or services.	☐ We see process expenses as essential investments.
Pair 5	☐ We focus on what our goals should be.	☐ We focus on how we should accomplish our goals.

Overall Rating
Using your above responses as a guide, mark an "X" in the box that best represents your workgroup or organization:

CONTENT	Mostly	More	Even	More	Mostly	PROCESS

Learning Orientation 3
Knowledge Reserve

Definition
Knowledge is possessed by individuals as compared to knowledge that is publicly available

Directions
For each pair, check the box that best describes your workgroup or organization.

	Personal	**Public**
Pair 1	☐ When we need knowledge, we turn to the person most expert in that domain.	☐ When we need knowledge, we turn to written or organized sources that would be found in a data bank or library.
Pair 2	☐ We believe that knowledge cannot always be stated in objective terms.	☐ We believe that knowledge can always be made explicit so that it is available to others.
Pair 3	☐ We rely on experts to keep track of what we know or do.	☐ We make every effort to document what we know or do.
Pair 4	☐ We put little stock in legends or myths about our history.	☐ We place great value on legends or myths about our history.
Pair 5	☐ To gather details about our history, we rely on what members of our team or business unit already know.	☐ We gather information about our history from written documents or photographs.

Overall Rating
Using your above responses as a guide, mark an "X" in the box that best represents your workgroup or organization:

PERSONAL	Mostly	More	Even	More	Mostly	PUBLIC

Learning Orientation 4
Dissemination Mode

Definition
Knowledge is shared in formal, prescribed methods as compared to knowledge that is shared through informal methods, such as role-modeling and casual interaction

Directions
For each pair, check the box that best describes your workgroup or organization.

	Formal	**Informal**
Pair 1	☐ We learn desired operational methods by using written procedure guidelines and manuals.	☐ We learn operational methods by verbally sharing knowledge between team or group members.
Pair 2	☐ When we have a new idea or method, we disseminate it in formal educational programs.	☐ When we have a new idea or method, a group of people embraces it and acts as role models.
Pair 3	☐ When we want something to change, leaders make a big coordinated effort to get this across to everyone.	☐ When we want to change something, our leaders cultivate a number of "champions" to spread the word.
Pair 4	☐ When we solve a problem or develop or provide a new service, we make formal announcements.	☐ When we solve a problem or develop or provide a new service, we don't formally announce it.
Pair 5	☐ When we add new members, they learn about our work through structured orientation programs.	☐ When new members are added, they learn about our work through their own efforts.

Overall Rating
Using your above responses as a guide, mark an "X" in the box that best represents your workgroup or organization:

FORMAL	Mostly	More	Even	More	Mostly	INFORMAL

Learning Orientation 5
Learning Scope

Definition
Preference for knowledge related to the improvement of existing products, services, or capabilities as compared to preference for knowledge related to the development of new ones

Directions
For each pair, check the box that best describes your workgroup or organization.

	Incremental	**Transformative**
Pair 1	☐ Our learning focuses on improving what we already know or do.	☐ Our learning focuses on matters that are completely new to us or lead us to reframe what we already know.
Pair 2	☐ We spend a great deal of time correcting or updating our procedures or work methods.	☐ We spend a great deal of time questioning the assumptions underlying our procedures or work methods.
Pair 3	☐ We use existing tools and methods when learning how to do things better.	☐ We focus on creating new methods when learning how to do things better.
Pair 4	☐ When things are going well, we tend to leave them as is.	☐ Even when things are going well, we think about change.

Overall Rating
Using your above responses as a guide, mark an "X" in the box that best represents your workgroup or organization:

INCREMENTAL	Mostly	More	Even	More	Mostly	TRANSFORMATIVE

Learning Orientation 6
Value–Chain Focus

Definition
Emphasis on learning investments in engineering or production activities
("design and make" functions) versus sales or service activities ("market
and deliver" functions)

Directions
For each pair, check the box that best describes your workgroup or
organization.

	Design-Make	**Market-Deliver**
Pair 1	☐ The quest for technical superiority outweighs everything.	☐ The quest for service to the customer outweighs everything.
Pair 2	☐ We are likely to collaborate or subcontract with organizations that design or assemble our products.	☐ We are likely to collaborate or subcontract with organizations that can market or deliver our products.
Pair 3	☐ We focus on developing skills needed to design and make products.	☐ We focus on developing skills to market and deliver products.
Pair 4	☐ Other firms are likely to want to benchmark with us in areas of "design and make" functions.	☐ Other firms are likely to want to benchmark with us in areas of "market and deliver" functions.

Overall Rating
Using your above responses as a guide, mark an "X" in the box that best
represents your workgroup or organization:

DESIGN-MAKE	Mostly	More	Even	More	Mostly	MARKET-DELIVER

Learning Orientation 7
Learning Focus

Definition
Development of knowledge and skills pertaining to individual performance as compared to the development of knowledge and skills pertaining to group performance

Directions
For each pair, check the box that best describes your workgroup or organization.

	Individual	**Group**
Pair 1	☐ We believe in the skills and decision-making abilities of individuals.	☐ We believe in what can be accomplished by teams and task forces.
Pair 2	☐ Our educational programs are primarily geared toward the development of individuals.	☐ Our educational programs are primarily geared toward the development of teams.
Pair 3	☐ Our recognition system is designed to reward individual learning and development.	☐ Our recognition system is designed to reward group learning and development.
Pair 4	☐ When we hire individuals, we are most interested in their ability to perform a specific function.	☐ When we hire individuals, we are most interested in their ability to work well with others.

Overall Rating
Using your above responses as a guide, mark an "X" in the box that best represents your workgroup or organization:

INDIVIDUAL	Mostly	More	Even	More	Mostly	GROUP

Making Sense of the Choices You've Made

The configuration of learning approaches you selected profiles that unit's Learning Orientations. In effect, the choices you have just made paint a picture of its learning style. Every team or organization has a distinctive style, whether that style developed through intentional, directed action or in some latent, undirected way. That style stems largely from the nature of your team's or organization's culture, and, like culture, is often invisible or taken for granted.

The picture you have painted is neither good nor bad; it simply reflects in aggregate what is. We could examine this part of the profile and make some judgements about its appropriateness, but the picture is not yet complete. Part 2 of the OLI is the focus of the next chapter.

Intervention Starts with the Assessment

In using diagnostic tools like the OLI, it is important to realize that diagnosis or assessment is itself a form of intervention. Making an assessment produces both intended and unintended effects, for when you collect the data required, you effectively start to intervene in that situation or system (Schein, 1999a). The reaction you provoke can have unanticipated or unintended consequences.

When you use, either by yourself or with colleagues, surveys or other obtrusive means to collect data, you raise expectations, hopes, and perhaps fears as well. For example, when you collect data from interviews or ask people to complete questionnaires, those respondents may readily think about why the survey or assessment is being done, how the results will get used, whether the findings will impact them, and whether the results might be misinterpreted. The very process of raising questions or asking people to reflect on their own behavior can lead them to rethink or reframe their world.

Group Learning Starts with Participatory Assessment

If learning is inherently social (Michalski, 1997), then involving staff in assessment can intensify the learning experience. The more people you engage in assessment or who use the OLI with you, the larger the intervention and the sooner you begin a group learning process. A participatory approach to assessment would also elicit team members' views about learning objectives and leverage points for change. Hence assessment and diagnosis become ways of learning about learning, and the generation of insight and the sharing of information about learning serve as interventions.

Learning Practices: Lesson 2

Assessment and diagnosis require behaviors and analysis that produce learning. When we directly involve our colleagues in assessment, we make it a social activity. One result is shared insight, the foundation for critical, valued action and change.

3

Assessing the Conditions for Learning: Facilitating Factors

Bad news must travel fast.
—Bill Gates

Organizational Learning Inventory, Part 2

Obtaining a complete picture of a team's or an organization's learning capability requires more than a description of its learning style. While a style is in place and some forms of learning naturally occur, most learning is not serendipitous. Specific initiatives can overcome the structural and systemic characteristics of organizations that may block or thwart learning efforts. For example, Ed Schein (1996) claims that cultural differences within organizations create innate barriers to learning and that anxiety about change can overwhelm the desire to learn (Schein, 1993). However, consistent with an OD or appreciative inquiry perspective, the focus needs to be on those factors that promote learning rather than constrain it, and assessment must consider how prevalent those conditions are.

This chapter meets that need by providing Part 2 of the OLI to guide you to an assessment of your team's or organization's Facilitating Factors. Table 3-1 describes a set of processes or practices that influence the ease with which learning occurs and the amount of learning that takes place. This set of 10 Facilitating Factors is based on my own research (Nevis, DiBella & Gould, 1995) and is consistent with the writing of others (Garvin, 1993; McGill, 1992; Senge, 1990; Watkins & Marsick, 1993).

The OLI contains a page for each of the 10 FFs. By completing this second part of the OLI, you generate 10 more data points, but these

Table 3-1
Facilitating Factors

Facilitating Factors are the processes or practices that promote learning. In general, the more these factors are present, the easier it will be for a team or organization to learn.

1. **Scanning Imperative**
   Gather information about conditions and practices outside one's own unit; seek out information about the external environment.
2. **Performance Gap**
   Shared perception of gap between current and desired performance.
3. **Concern for Measurement**
   Considerable effort is spent defining or measuring key factors; discourse over metrics is regarded as a learning activity.
4. **Organizational Curiosity**
   Curiosity about conditions and practices; interest in creative ideas and new technologies; support for experimentation.
5. **Climate of Openness**
   Open communication among organizational members; problems, errors, or lessons are shared, not hidden.
6. **Continuous Education**
   Commitment of quality resources for learning.
7. **Operational Variety**
   Value different methods, procedures, and competencies; appreciate diversity.
8. **Multiple Advocates**
   New ideas and methods can be advanced by employees at all organizational levels; multiple advocates or champions exist.
9. **Involved Leadership**
   Leaders are personally and actively involved in learning initiatives and in ensuring that a learning environment is maintained.
10. **Systems Perspective**
    Recognition of interdependence among organizational units and groups; awareness of time delay between actions and their outcomes.

---

are normative in nature. In general, the greater the amount of evidence of each factor, the greater the opportunity for learning to occur. Since every group or organization is in some ways unique, the criticality of each factor—and hence the leverage points to promote learning—will vary from group to group. In order to complete this part of the OLI, keep in mind the specific nature of the organizational unit you profiled in Chapter 2 and then review the following sections of each page:

Definition and Statements

A brief definition introduces each Facilitating Factor. Several statements that reflect how your workgroup or organization acts or values each factor follow.

Profiling Your Unit

Consider the degree to which your workgroup or organization emphasizes or is effective in each factor. Read the statements for each factor and think about your workgroup's or organization's experience with that factor. To what extent does your group act in a manner consistent with these statements?

Examples

In the examples section, write down any incidents, cases, or circumstances that come to mind as you read the statements.

Overall Rating

At the bottom of each page put an "X" in the box that best describes the amount of evidence supporting the factor.

Summary Profile

Enter your assessment of each of the Facilitating Factors on the learning profile template (Fig. 3-1) located at the end of this chapter.

_____

Making Sense of the Choices You've Made

The choices you've made and the data points they represent indicate how good your team or organization is in promoting conditions that encourage learning. In effect, these data indicate your team's learning potential. When these data are combined with your team's or organization's Learning Orientations, we have a complete picture of its learning profile. In the next chapter we examine how this profile can be analyzed and its significance interpreted.

Facilitating Factor 1:
Scanning Imperative

Definition
Gather information about conditions and practices outside one's own unit; seek out information about the external environment

Statements that reflect "Scanning Imperative"

- We devote time and resources to understand our business environment.

- We periodically ask clients and customers about their perceptions of our performance.

- We devote time to the study of developing trends in our industry or profession.

- Staff in our unit maintain contact with customers, suppliers, competitors, and the government in the areas where we do business.

- Information from the external environment provides opportunities for learning.

- Comparative studies of competitors or suppliers are used in setting standards.

Examples from Your Unit

_____

_____

_____

_____

Overall Rating
Using reactions to the above statements as a guide, place an "X" in the box that best describes your workgroup or organization.

Little Evidence to Support This Factor		Some Evidence to Support This Factor			Extensive Evidence to Support This Factor	
1	2	3	4	5	6	7

Facilitating Factor 2:
Performance Gap

Definition
Shared perception of gap between current and desired
performance

Statements that reflect "Performance Gap"

- Most members of our unit agree that performance could be improved.

- There is a general awareness that the current standards of perform- ance should be set higher.

- We craft visions for the future that extend beyond our current status.

- Performance shortfalls create opportunities for learning.

- Our personnel feel stressed over our need to do better.

Examples from Your Unit

_____

_____

_____

_____

Overall Rating
Using reactions to the above statements as a guide, place an "X" in the box
that best describes your workgroup or organization.

Little Evidence to Support This Factor		Some Evidence to Support This Factor			Extensive Evidence to Support This Factor	
1	2	3	4	5	6	7

Facilitating Factor 3:
Concern for Measurement

Definition
Considerable effort is spent defining or measuring key factors; discourse over metrics is regarded as a learning activity

Statements that reflect "Concern for Measurement"

- We value the process of measurement as a learning opportunity.
- We talk about the outcomes and impact of our work.
- We are accustomed to using feedback and evaluation of varying kinds.
- We try to measure tangible and intangible effects.
- Our group believes that if you can name a target for change, you can measure and evaluate performance aimed at achieving it.
- Communicating outcomes is an essential activity.

Examples from Your Unit

_____

_____

_____

_____

Overall Rating
Using reactions to the above statements as a guide, place an "X" in the box that best describes your workgroup or organization.

Little Evidence to Support This Factor		Some Evidence to Support This Factor			Extensive Evidence to Support This Factor	
1	2	3	4	5	6	7

Facilitating Factor 4:
Organizational Curiosity

Definition
Curiosity about conditions and practices; interest in creative ideas and new technologies; support for experimentation

Statements that reflect "Organizational Curiosity"

• We recognize and reward those who develop and try out new ideas, even when their actions lead to unexpected or negative results.

• We always try to understand how things work.

• We are receptive to unanticipated events and use them to learn.

• Members of our unit continually inquire into innovative and creative ideas.

• Asking questions is highly valued.

• Experimentation is encouraged.

• We often engage in brainstorming exercises.

Examples from Your Unit

_____

_____

_____

_____

Overall Rating
Using reactions to the above statements as a guide, place an "X" in the box that best describes your workgroup or organization.

Little Evidence to Support This Factor		Some Evidence to Support This Factor			Extensive Evidence to Support This Factor	
1	2	3	4	5	6	7

Facilitating Factor 5:
Climate of Openness

Definition
Open communication among organizational members; problems, errors, or lessons are shared, not hidden

Statements that reflect "Climate of Openness"

- There is widespread dissemination of critical information and performance indicators in our unit.

- Ideas are openly shared and can be discussed by all interested employees.

- New employees are given frequent opportunities to learn from others at all levels in the organization.

- We are structured so that teams working on similar tasks can readily share their experiences and problems.

- Errors or defects are treated as learning opportunities.

Examples from Your Unit

_____

_____

_____

_____

Overall Rating
Using reactions to the above statements as a guide, place an "X" in the box that best describes your workgroup or organization.

Little Evidence to Support This Factor		Some Evidence to Support This Factor			Extensive Evidence to Support This Factor	
1	2	3	4	5	6	7

Facilitating Factor 6:
Continuous Education

Definition
Commitment of quality resources for learning

Statements that reflect "Continuous Education"
- Everyone is encouraged to acquire new knowledge and expertise.
- We support education at all levels, ranging from basic skills to advanced professional development.
- Financial resources for education are routinely available in good times and bad.
- We are good at providing developmental, on-the-job experiences for our people.
- The value of education is demonstrated by rewards for employees who pursue appropriate training.

Examples from Your Unit

_____

_____

_____

_____

Overall Rating
Using reactions to the above statements as a guide, place an "X" in the box that best describes your workgroup or organization.

Little Evidence to Support This Factor		Some Evidence to Support This Factor			Extensive Evidence to Support This Factor	
1	2	3	4	5	6	7

Facilitating Factor 7:
Operational Variety

Definition
Value different methods, procedures, and competencies; appreciate diversity

Statements that reflect "Operational Variety"

• We do not insist that all sections of a unit follow the same work rules or use the same processes.

• Personnel policies are flexible and allow for differences in how work is done, the needs of different employee groups, and local customs.

• We hire people with differing educations, backgrounds, and work experiences.

• We view variety as an opportunity to be used, not as a problem to be managed away.

• In staffing workgroups, we consciously strive for a mix of people with diverse competencies and perspectives.

• We try to learn from one another regardless of individual differences in culture, gender, or learning style.

Examples from Your Unit

_____

_____

_____

_____

Overall Rating
Using reactions to the above statements as a guide, place an "X" in the box that best describes your workgroup or organization.

Little Evidence to Support This Factor		Some Evidence to Support This Factor			Extensive Evidence to Support This Factor	
1	2	3	4	5	6	7

Facilitating Factor 8:
Multiple Advocates

___

Definition
New ideas and methods can be advanced by employees at all organizational levels; multiple advocates or champions exist

Statements that reflect "Multiple Advocates"

- Individuals with new knowledge to share are rarely blocked by the pressure to conform.

- Grassroots efforts to promote new ideas and new areas of learning are encouraged.

- Initiatives from all staff are carefully considered.

- Employees share responsibility for developing new areas of learning; the task of understanding new issues is not simply delegated to specialists.

- When we need to implement truly significant changes, we usually develop multiple champions.

- It is not unusual to find people voluntarily sharing their experience.

Examples from Your Unit

___

___

___

___

Overall Rating
Using reactions to the above statements as a guide, place an "X" in the box that best describes your workgroup or organization.

Little Evidence to Support This Factor		Some Evidence to Support This Factor			Extensive Evidence to Support This Factor	
1	2	3	4	5	6	7

Facilitating Factor 9:
Involved Leadership

Definition
Leaders are personally and actively involved in learning initiatives and in ensuring that a learning environment is maintained

Statements that reflect "Involved Leadership"

- Leadership is encouraged at all levels.
- Leaders "walk their talk"; if they espouse an idea, they show it in their behavior by being good role models.
- When an educational program is introduced, top people participate as students.
- Leaders follow up on initiatives by making resources available or by removing barriers to learning.
- Leaders work hard to create language and other symbols that support a given vision, help focus our mission, and promote learning.
- Everyone is a teacher; everyone is a learner.

Examples from Your Unit

_____

_____

_____

_____

Overall Rating
Using reactions to the above statements as a guide, place an "X" in the box that best describes your workgroup or organization.

Little Evidence to Support This Factor		Some Evidence to Support This Factor			Extensive Evidence to Support This Factor	
1	2	3	4	5	6	7

Facilitating Factor 10:
Systems Perspective

Definition
Recognition of interdependence among organizational units and groups; awareness of time delay between actions and their outcomes

Statements that reflect "Systems Perspective"

- We recognize that our long-term performance is related to the performance of others.

- We have a long-range perspective; we do not make changes based simply upon our current abilities or activities.

- When making a significant change in one part of our operations, we give considerable attention to the potential impact of the change on other parts.

- When we experience performance problems, we are more likely to examine our internal activities than we are to attribute our problems to external factors.

- We are suspicious of explanations of problems that rely on a single factor.

Examples from Your Unit

_____

_____

_____

_____

Overall Rating
Using reactions to the above statements as a guide, place an "X" in the box that best describes your workgroup or organization.

Little Evidence to Support This Factor		Some Evidence to Support This Factor			Extensive Evidence to Support This Factor	
1	2	3	4	5	6	7

Figure 3-1
Template for Facilitating Factors

FACILITATING FACTORS:	Little Evidence to Support This Factor		Some Evidence to Support This Factor			Extensive Evidence to Support This Factor	
	1	2	3	4	5	6	7
1. Scanning Imperative							
2. Performance Gap							
3. Concern for Measurement							
4. Organizational Curiosity							
5. Climate of Openness							
6. Continuous Education							
7. Operational Variety							
8. Multiple Advocates							
9. Involved Leadership							
10. Systems Perspective							

Learning Practices: Lesson 3

Learning is not just serendipitous but requires resources and focused investment. Assessing the conditions for learning means looking at what can promote both intentional and serendipitous learning.

4

Recognizing Your "Best Possible" Learning Profile

When the guru points to the moon,
the fool sees only a finger.
—Anthony DeMello

The purpose of this chapter is to outline ways of analyzing your team's or organization's learning profile and recognizing a more preferred one. This chapter makes the bridge to Step 2 of an OD approach (See Figure 4-1), to building learning capability by creating the vision for a more desirable or strategic profile. That vision, when compared to current reality, establishes a gap between existing learning processes and strategic learning needs. The discrepancy between what is and what might be creates the tension needed to stimulate change (Beckhard & Harris, 1987).

Figure 4-1
OD Approach to Build Organizational Learning Capability

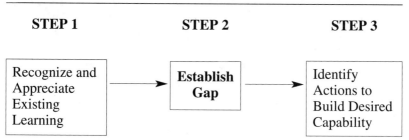

STEP 1	STEP 2	STEP 3
Recognize and Appreciate Existing Learning	**Establish Gap**	Identify Actions to Build Desired Capability

An Up-Front Word About Process

In using the OLI in workshops with personnel from a variety of organizations, I have come to anticipate questions such as: Do we have the best profile? What should our profile be? How does our profile compare with that of our competitors? These questions naturally arise as a group develops its profile. As soon as the profile is complete, group members evaluate or make some sense of it. These may be the very questions you are asking yourself, now that you have completed a learning profile. Underlying such questions is often a presumption that there is one best profile and that if we knew what it was, then everything else would be easy, including the success that would surely follow.

There are three problems with this presumption. First, the notion that any organizational unit has a singular profile does not take into account that team and organizational learning is a pluralistic capability. A profile for a large organizational unit is a composite of multiple profiles of smaller constituent units. The focus, therefore, should not be on a single profile but on understanding what that profile represents and how it may compare to, complement, or conflict with the profiles of related units.

Second, knowing what a profile should look like in theory is not the same as implementing a set of actions and behaviors that establish the profile in reality. A theoretically optimal answer is worthless if it can't be realized. Taking organizational action or fixing systemic problems is far more complex than changing a lightbulb. Another liability in relying on theoretically derived solutions is that their appropriateness can disappear over time as the context changes or as theory evolves. For example, at one point in the development of management thought, companies were told to "stick to their knitting" (Peters & Waterman, 1982), but in changing times that is the last thing a company should do lest it suffer the consequences of myopia (Levitt, 1960).

Finally, there is a presumption that knowing the answer, or the right profile, is more important than the process whereby the answer was developed or recognized, or in other words, that the end is more important than the means. In his book *The Rise and Fall of Strategic Planning* (1994), Henry Mintzberg points out that the process of strategic planning is as critical, if not more so, as the outcomes of that process. Among the reasons for this claim is that how strategic plans are developed can have a more lasting impact than do such plans themselves. (Another management thinker, Karl Weick [1988], has suggested that having a map can be more important than the accuracy of the map itself.) Knowing a right answer is often less important than having a way to use what you know. A so-called "best solution" that can't be implemented is not as good as one that can be.

Thus, the question "What is the best profile for an organizational unit?" is not the best one to raise. What is more critical is asking how the desired profile will be identified, which in effect is a question about process. How you or your team comes to identify your desired profile is as important as the nature of that profile itself and reflects how you, as a manager, internal or external consultant, or facilitator, relate to your client organization. Are you an expert at dispensing advice or prescriptions (doctor–patient) or a counselor who helps people help themselves (learner–process consultant)? (For a detailed discussion of these roles, see Schein 1987, 1999a.)

A Consultant Dilemma

As convinced as I am that providing pat answers and prescriptions does not make for meaningful, long-term change in a client system, I am often confronted in my consulting engagements with companies who expect that of me. Most managers are willing to pay for expert solutions but not for expert process, and when looking to build learning capability in their teams or organizations, they usually seek a blueprint. "Just tell us what to do" is the standard refrain. The OD consultant who wants to be process oriented yet customer focused (and market successful!) is thus put in a difficult position.

There are three ways by which I have come to finesse my way through this dilemma:

- Focus on Criteria
- Work with the Data
- Provide Structure

It is essential to get the client organization to focus on itself rather than on the consultant's advice, and these three tasks have a way of subtly doing just that.

1. Focus on Criteria
How would we know a better profile if we saw it? What would be the characteristics of a desired best profile? If clients want to know their best profile, it's reasonable to ask them about criteria and what they

want to achieve from developing learning capability. In effect, the issue pertains to what performance measures a team, organization, or company monitor and how establishing a better learning profile might impact those measures.

Building learning capability is not an end unto itself. Presumably, moving a team or organization toward a preferred profile would positively impact whatever ends the team or organization is trying to achieve. Learning requires some investment in time, personnel, and other resources so questions such as why invest in learning and what outcomes are to be expected are not insignificant. Knowing what those ends are and what criteria or measures the team uses to assess performance are essential prerequisites to a successful intervention. Small group discussions to identify learning and performance outcomes and their measures are a straightforward way to move the process along and to get teams and organizations to reflect on what they need to achieve.

2. Work with the Data

Another simple yet powerful way to transparently focus the discussion away from a prescriptive best profile is to start with the data. In creating a learning profile, a team has in effect created 17 data points. These points can be looked at individually, in groups (LOrs versus FFs), or in aggregate as a type of gestalt. In effect, we can ask the client to analyze and reflect on their current profile. In working with multiple teams from the same organization, we can look at the data in terms of each team's distinctive profile and the similarities and differences between teams. The latter can serve as an interesting basis for a discussion of intergroup differences, whether they are sources of conflict or collaboration.

This reflection can be organized around a series of general questions such as:

> Which Facilitating Factors were rated highest or lowest?
>
> Are there any extreme data points, either 1s or 7s on Facilitating Factors or "mostly" positions on Learning Orientations?
>
> How does the profile of one team differ from or complement the profiles of other teams?
>
> How did the composition of the team affect the profile that was generated?

Are any of the data points surprising, disappointing, or affirming?

Learning Orientations

Individual data points can be discussed in terms of how they represent a team's values or contribute to achieving a team's mission or performance goals. For example, if a team's Value–Chain Focus (LOr 6) is mostly "Design-Make," might that point out insufficient attention is being paid to customer or client concerns? If a team relies heavily on personal Knowledge Reserve (LOr 3), does that suggest a lack of emphasis on institutionalized knowledge?

Examination of the data could also include a review of relative positions on the seven Learning Orientations. Statistical analyses of profiles I have collected indicate that the correlations between the seven LOrs are close to zero, meaning that each LOr is independent of the others and that each represents a unique dimension of organizational learning capability. Relationships between LOrs can be looked at to identify different learning styles (DiBella, 1996). For example, when Knowledge Source (LOr 1, "internal" versus "external") is juxtaposed with Learning Scope (LOr 5, "incremental" versus "transformative"), the result (see Fig. 4-2) is a 2 × 2 matrix of four learning styles: correction (internal Knowledge Source and incremental Learning Scope), innovation (internal Knowledge Source and transformative Learning Scope), adaptation (external Knowledge Source and incremental Learning Scope), and acquisition (external Knowledge Source

Figure 4-2
Styles of Learning as Reflected By Knowledge Source and Learning Scope

| | | Learning Scope | |
		Incremental	Transformative
Knowledge Source	**External**	adaptation	acquisition
	Internal	correction	innovation

and transformative Learning Scope). A team's profile data can be matched up against this matrix.

Facilitating Factors

One approach to the data on Facilitating Factors, which reflect or create conditions essential for learning, is to identify their relative importance for the team or organization. Social systems promote learning in different ways and for different reasons. Analysis of aggregate data can be used to create coefficients that represent how important each FF is on average across a large number of groups or profiles. However, every team or group has its own idiosyncrasies. Hence, the criticality of each Facilitating Factor will vary within and between teams. From a systems thinking point of view, it is helpful to identify which FFs serve as leverage points for change in particular groups and then to consider the team's relative strength or capability in that area.

One tool to recognize whether the relative amount of a team's FFs is in balance with its criticality is to create a plot-diagram of factor significance (Fig. 4-3). This exercise requires a ranking of the relative importance of the 10 FFs. This ranking is then plotted against the profile data for FF. The ideal result would be an upwardly curving line or a straight line with a positive slope. Either result would suggest that the team has strong capabilities in those FFs that count most. If the shape of the plotted data deviates from the ideal result, that would indicate that there are factors a team should work on for maximum effect.

Figure 4-3
Plot of Significance of Factor by Evidence

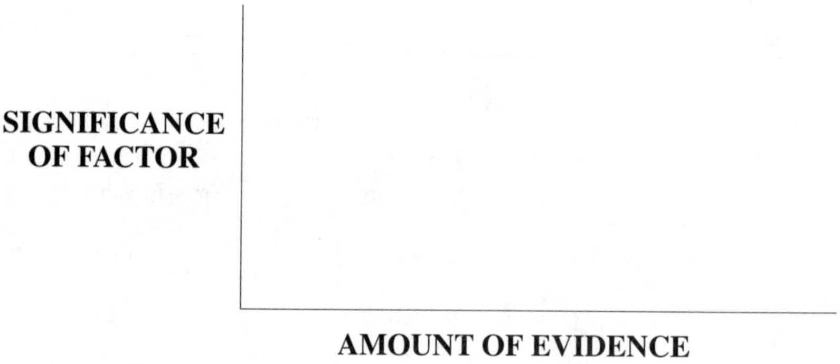

SIGNIFICANCE
OF FACTOR

AMOUNT OF EVIDENCE

Overall Pattern

Finally, it's possible to look at the overall pattern of the profile as well as the relationship between the LOrs and the FFs. Analysis of profile data I have collected indicates that teams have a tendency to rate themselves high or low on the FFs. That is, many teams consistently rate themselves high on all the FFs or consistently low. This trend may suggest some synergy between the FFs: that teams high on some FFs are apt to be equally high on the other FFs. It may also reflect a bias in the profiling process whereby some teams are overly critical or overly lenient in their self-assessment.

As a check on the reliability of the data, data points on the FFs can be compared with data from the LOrs. For example, a team that rates itself "1" or "2" on Scanning Imperative should have a mostly internal Knowledge Source. A team that has little evidence in the domain of Multiple Advocates (FF 8) is likely to have an individual approach to Learning Focus (LOr 7).

In a framework of 17 elements there are multiple points of comparison that can spawn a series of conversations and reflections. That process becomes richer and more complicated when you work with multiple units (and hence multiple profiles) from the same organization. In that context comparisons can be made between different profiles, as well as within individual ones.

3. Provide Structure

While process and OD consultants shun giving answers or providing solutions, many of our clients look to us for guidance in trying to figure out what our models mean or in what they need to do. It may be inappropriate to dole out content, but it's equally inappropriate to run away from a client's need to help them move along in their process. One way to resolve this dilemma is to provide structure for a client's deliberations and reflections. The idea behind providing structure is reflected in the following quote attributed to the ancient Chinese philosopher Lao Tzu:

> From damp clay molded into place, a vessel may be wrought;
> And yet for its empty space, its value would be nought.

Structure and consultant tools provide the "container" for client input and reflection. (In effect, the learning profile format is such a tool.) One way I have structured client reflection on their learning profile is to turn the conversation toward the critical link between learning capability and strategic direction: Given a company's strategy, what are

Chart 4-1

Learning Implications of Strategy

Strategic Components	What Needs to Be Learned?	Who Needs to Learn?	How Will Learning Occur?
1.	a.	a1, a2, a3...	a1i, a1ii, a2i...
	b.	b1, b2, b3...	b1i, b1ii, b2i...
	c.		
	d.		
2.	a.	a1, a2, a3...	a1i, a1ii, a2i...
	b.	b1, b2, b3...	b1i, b1ii, b2i...
	c.		
	d.		
3.	a.	a1, a2, a3...	a1i, a1ii, a2i...
	b.	b1, b2, b3...	b1i, b1ii, b2i...
	c.		
	d.		
4.	a.	a1, a2, a3...	a1i, a1ii, a2i...
	b.	b1, b2, b3...	b1i, b1ii, b2i...
	c.		
	d.		
5.	a.	a1, a2, a3...	a1i, a1ii, a2i...
	b.	b1, b2, b3...	b1i, b1ii, b2i...
	c.		
	d.		

the learning implications, what needs to be learned, and how will that learning occur? Chart 4-1 provides a format ("container" or "vessel") to organize or structure a client's reflection on these strategic issues.

For an organization or firm to implement its strategy, there are critical learning implications, especially when companies change their strategy. New strategies often require new skills or new ways for employees to work together. Given the strategy, exactly what do employees need to learn or know for the strategy to be successful? Completing Chart 4-1 requires first an elaboration of a firm's strategy into discrete components, or areas of emphasis or direction (column 1). Then for each component, we list what needs to be learned—be it skills or behavior, knowledge or insight, attitudes or emotions—and who needs to acquire such learning (columns 2 and 3). Finally, we specify how such learning will take place (column 4). This latter task brings the focus back to the learning profile in either affirming the appropriateness of current learning approaches or suggesting the need for new ones.

Table 4-1 is an abbreviated example of using this structure to make the connection between learning and strategy and to capture the results from such an exercise.

The principle behind using structures or formats like Chart 4-1 is that it gets a team to be task or content focused—the task being to complete the form. The secret to the value of this exercise is that the process of completing the form engages team members or company employees in conversations about their learning. Such conversations inevitably raise questions and generate insight about a firm's strategy, the link between strategy and learning, and the appropriateness of current learning approaches.

Table 4-1
Learning Implications of Strategy, Example

Strategic Components	What Needs to Be Learned?	Who Needs to Learn?	How Will Learning Occur?
Become more customer friendly	How to better manage the trade-off between customer focus and length of call	Call-center staff	Formal dissemination via classroom training Role-modeling on the job

Profiles: "Better" and "Best Possible"

The aim of these three tasks (Focus on Criteria, Work with the Data, Provide Structure) is to increase consciousness about learning issues. That sensitivity is a prerequisite to developing a "better" or "best possible" learning profile for which the group or team has a sense of ownership. Better profiles are those that enhance the conditions or practices (FFs) that promote learning or align what gets learned with the strategic needs of the team or organization.

For those organizations undergoing some type of culture change, LOrs need to shift so that new learning processes align with the new culture. For example, organizations with cultures that place a high value on individuals or independent, entrepreneurial action are apt to emphasize personal Knowledge Reserve and individual Learning Focus as modes of learning. If such companies wish to develop work environments that are more oriented toward groups or collaborative work, then their LOrs need to shift to reinforce those transitions. Hence Learning Focus would shift toward a group approach, and Knowledge Reserve would shift toward a public approach.

Certain things in life are easier said than done; it is one thing to identify or talk about a better learning profile for a team, organization, or company, but realizing that profile is something altogether different. The credibility of change is a delicate matter that builds on success. Consequently, the distinction between what's best and "best possible" is not trivial but relates to the need to develop reasonable expectations.

The reason that many efforts to build learning organizations fail is that they overlook the fact that all social or collective units, workgroups, teams, organizations, and companies have preexisting and embedded learning processes. Learning practices that are inconsistent with a unit's learning profile will meet resistance; others that conform to that profile will be accepted more readily. Thus in considering ways to improve a team's learning profile, we need to take into account what fits the culture and is therefore possible versus what requires a significant transformation in underlying values or assumptions.

"Best Possible" Profile: Process Issues

This text is not a guidebook to changing organization culture; that topic has been well addressed elsewhere (see, for example, Schein 1992, 1999b). However, it would be folly to talk about changing

Learning Orientations without recognizing that some sort of culture shift is involved. The more extensive that shift, the more difficult the transition and the greater the need to broaden staff participation in developing a desired profile.

In the process of developing their profile of existing capabilities, groups inevitably discuss how their profile differs from what it may have been in the past, what they think it should be in the future, and whether it may be shifting. This shared insight provides a starting point for groups to conduct action planning on ways to expand learning capability. Once a gap between current and desired learning capability has been established, the group can identify learning practices that focus on learning issues. The key is to let the group's own knowledge about the potentialities and leverage points for change guide the action planning process. Instead of imposing a solution for developing learning capability, a facilitator would prompt the group to come up with its own problem definition (as reflected in the gap between the current and desired profiles) and its own solution (action plans). In this way, the outcome will be a set of interventions that has group ownership and builds upon the group's own knowledge.

"Best Possible" Profile: Content Issues

The content of a learning profile can be looked at in two distinctive ways: by itself and in comparison to profiles from units in the same organization or company. That is, while each profile can and does stand on its own, its properties need to be considered within its larger context. Each perspective has different implications for improving learning capability and thus for establishing a "best possible" profile.

Although a team's learning processes are embedded in its culture, culture is not the sole determinant of those processes or of a team's learning profile. Rather, they stem from a variety of factors including:

- Nature of Work Transactions
- Identifiability of Learning Opportunities
- Implications of Learning Outcomes
- Rewards
- Interdependencies

Each of these properties of a work system affects what types of knowledge are acquired, disseminated, shared, and how. Discussions centered around these properties promote awareness and sensitivity about desired learning capability.

1. Nature of Work Transactions

Most any form of work, especially in the postindustrial era, requires some learned skill or level of knowledge. Many jobs today involve some amount of information processing or knowledge sharing. In either case, how workers use knowledge and information and where they get it represent learning processes that are directly related to the nature of work itself. For example, in financial service firms and catalog retailers, customer service staff must learn how to process customer transactions. At computer software and hardware "800" support lines, technicians must have the knowledge to problem-solve and shared mechanisms to store and retrieve information about generic problems and their solutions.

Diversity in work tasks means variations between what type of knowledge is needed, where the knowledge comes from, and how knowledge is acquired. When members of a workgroup reflect on the nature of their desired learning profile, it's critical that they keep in mind the essence of the work they do and their performance demands. There are many ways to redesign what a group learns and how, but unless such changes create value by increasing desirable outcomes, the resources required of learning (time, money, personnel) will be allocated elsewhere. A good way to focus group discussion on this issue is to ask about the learning that needs to occur in order for the performance of that group to improve.

2. Identifiability of Learning Opportunities

From their collective efforts workgroups and companies create identifiable outcomes or specific products or services. Along the way they also have experiences, pass certain milestones, or realize points of progress. Each of these milestones, outcomes, or events provides opportunities for reflection and potential learning. Some, like intermediate goals, are anticipated; others, like accidents or failures, are not. Erecting a new building, for example, is a potential learning event for a construction company, as is every claim processed by an insurance company, every movie made by a film company, every game played by a professional (and amateur) sports team, every flight of a commercial airline, or every new product developed by a consumer goods firm.

Learning events can derive from failure as well as from success, as when a team loses a critical game, a new product flops on the market (New Coke, Edsel), or operations go terribly wrong (Three Mile Island nuclear accident, *Challenger* space shuttle disaster, Union Carbide gas explosion in Bhopal). The first step in developing a capability to use experience (success or failure) is having a shared recognition of what constitutes a learning event for a particular workgroup, company, or industry. This can lead a group to establish processes to analyze and learn from such events.

Learning from critical, identifiable events is not restricted to one's own experience. Teams and companies also benefit when they replicate someone else's success or don't repeat their own mistakes. For example, while the French nuclear power industry learns from the operating experience of their own plants, they were also able to learn from the United States' experience at Three Mile Island. What the National Transportation Safety Board learns from one airplane crash ultimately benefits all airlines and passengers. Discussing how or whether teams recognize and process learning events can provide insight into a more desirable learning profile.

3. Implications of Learning Outcomes

A popular caveat in the legal profession is that in the courtroom an attorney should never ask a witness a question to which the attorney doesn't already know the answer. When we step into uncharted territory, there's uncertainty about where we might end up. When we invest in learning, we can never be sure of the payoff. If that payoff can have disastrous implications, then we need to be very careful about what and how we hope to learn. Workgroups or companies that function in contexts in which poor performance can lead to harmful or disastrous circumstances must be very selective in their learning approaches.

For example, one of the work settings whose learning properties I studied was the control room in several nuclear power plants. The complex interactions and tightly coupled nature of the systems at a nuclear power plant means that minor missteps can produce expected or so-called "normal" accidents (Perrow, 1984). Consequently, transformative Learning Scope is an approach that should not be part of the daily repertoire of activities in a control room or in the cockpit of a commercial airliner. (In fact, the nuclear accident at Chernobyl occurred when engineers tried to experiment with maintaining electrical output even as the reactor was being shut down.)

Transformative Learning Scope, Organizational Curiosity, Operational Variety, or learning through experimentation are conditions and practices that should not be promoted in the day-to-day operation of high-reliability organizations (Roberts & Gargano, 1990). On the other hand, these may be the very skills or practices that can help a team avoid disaster when tried-and-true methods for learning don't solve an impending crisis. In that case the team must be able to switch styles.

For example, in 1989 United Airlines Flight 232 lost all hydraulic fluid, which meant that the aircraft (a DC-10) could not be steered through instrumentation. This situation had never been imagined by the architects of the DC-10 or by flight trainers. Thus the crew faced a situation for which they had never been trained and for which there were no procedures to follow. What enabled Flight 232 to crashland in a Sioux City, Iowa, cornfield with minimal loss of life was the capability of the crew to learn transformatively and develop a way to steer the plane manually.

Choosing a learning approach is dependent not only on the timeliness of using what is learned, but also on its significance. For example, when a sick patient is facing imminent death, caregivers (doctors or nurses) often use new or experimental protocols or procedures. Such practices are not learned a priori but in their doing. Here the risk of inaction (loss of the patient) outweighs the possibility that the caregiver may improperly administer the new technique or procedure. Figure 4-4 shows how certain learning approaches can be considered in light of the consequences of inaction and of their immediacy.

Figure 4-4
Fit Between Selected Learning Styles and Circumstances

		Consequences	
		Low	**High**
Timeframe	**Immediate**	Learning-in-Action	Transformative Learning Scope
	Long-Term	Incremental Learning Scope	Learning Through Simulation

4. Rewards

The payoff from learning investments can take place in the short or long term; the relevance of what gets learned can also vary. Hence certain types of learning (design-make versus market-deliver Value–Chain Focus; individual versus group Learning Focus) can be more useful to some teams than to others, especially to make that learning strategically aligned. Considerations of a desired learning profile must critically examine what value a team places on certain performance outcomes as reflected in its reward structure.

What a team or company rewards serves as a channel that guides learning investments. As an organization's reward systems go, so too will its learning investments. Thus, reflecting on a desired learning profile requires an examination of the team's or organization's reward systems—what gets rewarded, how often, and how large the rewards are relative to the cost of learning investments.

5. Interdependencies

The focus in the preceeding four issues has been a singular profile as generated by a particular team or organization. Another important way to consider the properties of a desired profile is to place that process in the context of a larger unit or an entire company. Rather than look at the specific features of an individual profile, we instead take a systems view and look at the relationship of a given profile to the context in which it is embedded.

When features of a profile are looked at in relationship to the profiles of related units, it's possible to recognize synergies or complementarities between them. For example, while we don't expect to see much transformative learning taking place in the control room of a nuclear power plant, we might expect control room staff to receive team (group Learning Focus) training on plant simulators. Meanwhile, in the same utility company or power plant, we would expect or want to see test engineers working in laboratories where they can perform experiments on equipment or modeled systems. In that context the unknown, potentially negative outcomes of learning would have no deleterious effects. The insights from lab experiments would complement the deliberate, incremental learning within operational settings.

Given the nature of the team's work tasks and learning implications as just discussed, particular team learning profiles might exhibit extreme characteristics (ratings such as "mostly"). When the profiles from complementary teams are combined in some larger aggregation, we would expect the resultant group profile to exhibit properties that are more "even" or balanced. The sum of different styles expands the learning capability of the larger unit and offsets some of the constraints faced by units whose work makes certain forms of learning inappropriate or unfeasible.

Recognizing Your "Best Possible" Learning Profile

In this chapter we have reviewed a variety of process and content issues that go into the development of a team's or company's "best possible" learning profile. What should be clear by now is that while there is no set formula, there are principles to follow. Team facilitators, whether internal or external, need to apply them in a manner that suits their role and their personal approach.

Having followed the principles described in this chapter, you or your team can now complete the second step in building learning capability—creating a desired learning profile—and thereby establish a gap between existing learning and strategic learning needs. In effect, whoever produced the initial profile revisits the framework of 17 elements and creates a second set of data points. These data points can be posted on the same template as the profile of current capability using a different marker. In Chapter 1, letters were used but any color, shape, letter, or numbered marker that distinguishes between current and desired capability will do. In aggregate, the additional data reflect the team's vision of its "best possible" profile. Part 2 describes a series of choices that teams and organizations face in order to make that vision a reality.

Learning Practices: Lesson 4

How we behave and interact with others can have a more significant impact than what we say. The best learning profile for any team or organization may simply be what its members can create and act upon together.

Part II

Learning Choices, Learning Interventions

Having created profile data using the OLI and then reflected on their meaning, we now make the transition from diagnosis to planned action. Uncovering existing learning capability is a prerequisite to determining how current capabilities can be modified or enhanced. Part II considers the array of learning choices that teams and companies need make to proactively create strategic capability. In aggregate, learning choices represent investments that support a learning infrastructure or architecture. Some of these choices (whether manifest or latent) are made at a group level and involve specific behaviors and practices. These choices are covered in Chapter 5, which describes ways to improve or alter LOrs, and in Chapter 6, which looks at how FFs can be intensified. Other choices involve learning that depends upon coordinated action or knowledge sharing between multiple groups or teams; Chapter 7 examines the practices that relate to this type of application.

5

Ways to Enhance or Shift Learning Orientations

Learning how to learn is life's most important skill.
—Tony Buzan

With profiles of current and desired learning capability (the latter presumably aligned with strategic directions) in hand, we now turn to making a desired profile a reality. This chapter (and the next) make the bridge to Step 3 of an OD approach to building learning capability (Fig. 5-1) by identifying the actions required to establish a more desirable or more strategic profile. In this chapter we specifically look at ways to either improve current learning approaches or shift them.

With seven Learning Orientations and altogether 14 distinctive learning approaches, there are a variety of methods that can be used to

Figure 5-1
OD Approach to Build Organizational Learning Capability

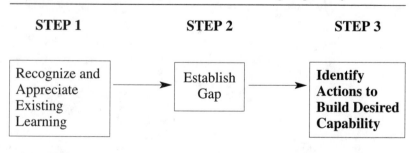

STEP 1	**STEP 2**	**STEP 3**
Recognize and Appreciate Existing Learning	Establish Gap	**Identify Actions to Build Desired Capability**

focus change actions. Some actions affect specific LOrs, or learning approaches, while others may change several LOrs all at once. We will first consider the latter, a collective or generic emphasis, and then the former, a singular or particular emphasis.

Focusing on a Collective Set of Learning Orientations

Increase or Alter Benefits from Existing Learning Events

Many organizations have naturally occurring activities and happenings that can produce learning. In the previous chapter I referred to these activities as "learning events" or "learning opportunities." An organization's own learning events represent internal Knowledge Source, while the recognized events of others represent external Knowledge Source. Either way, organizational experiences provide a potentially rich harvest of learning, but many organizations fail to benefit from them. There are several reasons why.

First, some organizational experiences are based in work routines that over time become transparent and undervalued. Completed projects and assignments are part of everyday work, and as soon as one is over, another is sure to follow. A cultural value of focusing on the future or the present leads to an undervaluing of the past. As soon as we finish one project or have some experience, we move onto the next without having recognized the inherent learning value of the experience we have just completed.

Second, when past events are acknowledged, it's usually because they have been categorized as successes or failures. Reflection on the past often leads to some sort of quick assessment or evaluation rather than analysis, which means that our emotions and feelings become engaged rather than our thoughts. Experiences considered "successful" make us feel good. As we appreciate them, we bask in their glory. These feelings reduce our performance anxiety and give us the misleading impression that one successful experience necessarily begets another. Instead of analyzing why things went right, we tend to relax; rather than invest resources in learning about how to replicate our successes, we simply go on to the next project or activity.

So-called "unsuccessful" experiences are an entirely different matter. They make us feel bad or defensive. Given the pressures of presentation of self (Goffman, 1959), we are apt to avoid, or worse, cover up experiences or events that might be viewed as failures, accidents, or mistakes that derive from incompetence. The litigious nature of our society can penalize organizations that come forward and acknowledge incompetence. Consequently, opportunities to learn from activities that produced undesirable results and to reduce their frequency are often not taken advantage of. Rather than reflecting on so-called failures, analyzing them, and rectifying their underlying causes, the tendency is often to avoid or forget them.

Finally, many people are simply unable to acknowledge how they might benefit from the experiences of others. One of the most intriguing and frustrating, yet recurrent themes I encounter in consulting across different industries and among different companies is every individual's and every company's sense of their own uniqueness. "That could never happen here," "they're different from us," and "that doesn't apply to us" are common refrains I hear when using case material on learning. Everyone thinks that they or their situation is so special that this belief in uniqueness overshadows the reality of commonality. They presume that what applies to one does not apply to another, and there is little or no appreciation for how one team or company might learn from the experiences of another.

Here are four ways to reharvest or increase the learning benefits from existing events and experiences:

- Develop Shared Recognition of Value
- Establish or Alter the Reflection Process
- Improve Utilization
- Increase Frequency

1. Develop Shared Recognition of Value

Many of us undervalue what we ourselves know or do or what others do. Consequently, we don't recognize the significance of our experiences and are unable to stand back or away from them to analyze their importance. Appreciative inquiry is an OD technique that encourages reflection from the position that a glass can be half full but never half empty, that there are as many if not more positive aspects of any situation as there are negative ones (Srivastva, 1999). By taking such a perspective, we come to value our past and present experiences, our current capabilities, and our potential.

However, to benefit from events and experiences as sources to promote learning in a team or organizational context requires collective or shared appreciation. When individuals by themselves take an appreciative view, others may see this as a boastful or self-congratulatory act, especially when they are concerned with the competitive implications. Recognizing the potential learning value of events and then reflecting on them must be shared through routine procedures and forms of behavior. Employees need to communicate to one another the benefits of learning from events in order to replicate the successful ones and avoid the unsuccessful. A sense of empathy can contribute to this potential. When we realize that our similarities are more substantial than our differences, we are more apt to identify with the experiences of others and hence benefit from them. Making employees aware of events and milestones makes everything more publicly visible and accessible.

2. Establish or Alter the Reflection Process

The day after a collegiate or professional sports game is the day when the players and coaches visit the videotape room. (Players on the famed Boston Celtics used to call one of their coaches, Bill Fitch, "Captain Video" because of his compulsion to spend countless hours with his team to analyze and learn from videotape.) The ability of sports teams and individual athletes to film their performances, and then use the tape to analyze and learn from their discrete experience may seem unique. Yet that ability represents a socially recognized effort to reflect on past experiences and to do so in an organized and almost routine manner.

Work teams and organizations similarly need and can benefit from capturing their experiences (collecting the data on behavior), analyzing those data, and sharing the insights gained therefrom. The first step is to establish some container for collecting data on organizational experience, either routinely over time or retrospectively. The duration of most organizational events and experiences is so lengthy as to make videotaping unfeasible (not to mention in potential conflict with privacy issues), but some way to gather data is essential. In effect, teams or organizations need some mechanism that parallels the presence on aircraft of a flight data recorder and voice cockpit recorder that record critical flight information (such as airspeed and elevation) and cockpit conversation. In this regard it is interesting to note the increasing practice by callcenters of taping the phone conversations between customers and call-center representatives.

When events can't be monitored and data can't be recorded instantaneously, then methods to collect data post facto must be put into place. Organizations may choose from an established set of social science data collection methods, such as surveys, panel or focus groups, and interviews. Some methods, such as learning histories (Roth, 1998), oral histories (Yow, 1994), and program evaluation (Suchman, 1967; Rossi, 1999), in effect combine data collection and interpretation.

Once the data are captured or an experience synthesized, companies need to set aside time from operational activities to make some collective sense of the past. In effect, teams and organizations need to conduct their own debriefing sessions and to realize that this "time out" is not "time off." A debrief is conducted in order to understand and benefit from past successes and failures. The frequency of these sessions can be tied to the calendar or to the internal cycle of socially recognized events or experiences. Organizations with continuous activities, such as manufacturing cycles, would probably conduct briefing sessions linked to some critical reporting period, such as a day, week, month, quarter, or year. Organizations with more discrete but infrequent activities might conduct briefings when critical milestones of an event or project are completed or reached. For example, a consumer product firm could debrief a new product development cycle or some marketing or advertising initiative; construction firms can debrief each building project.

Who participates in debriefing sessions and the process whereby they are conducted is critical to the learning experience. Unless an environment that fosters learning is established and unless the right "learners" are present, a debrief can easily fail to be an abundant harvest. Defensiveness can set in and analysis and interpretation can go awry when the experience or event being debriefed conflicts with preexisting beliefs or vested interests. One dominant principle or ground rule of debriefing should be that team members are not penalized for their mistakes but are held accountable for failing to change or learn from them. To avoid replicating mistakes or failing to learn from the past requires follow-up methods and ways to apply lessons learned.

3. Improve Utilization

Debriefing past events may generate lessons from experience, but it does not ensure the application of those lessons. The challenge is especially great when new knowledge conflicts with existing behaviors or routines or requires coordinated action by a set of stakeholders. Once lessons are generated, the focus must shift to issues of application and utilization. I have participated in many meetings where despite everyone's best intentions, the inertia of change overwhelms the desire to integrate lessons learned into operational procedures or routines.

While it is important to debrief our experiences, learning does not occur until we translate lessons into action. Learning is demonstrated only in or through action when we have indeed internalized our experience. (When learning only represents the potential for action, we can never truly *know* what we have learned since the proof is in the doing.) Many organizations try to jump-start, or ensure, utilization by creating written plans of action. Planning documents are helpful in specifying who needs to do what as a result of a debriefing. However, without a coordinated effort, plans do not necessarily lead to action, so there is always the need for follow-up.

A major reason for this failure to act is that after debriefing sessions staff refocus on their day-to-day responsibilities and simply forget or fail to make time for follow-up. Teams and organizations need to have ordained learning "champions" who can keep staff focused and aware of what needs to change as a result of some debriefing. "Champions" need to find ways to help staff assimilate new knowledge or knowledge that conflicts with existing patterns of thought or behavior. It is important to recognize that utilization of experience is an intervention that, to be successful, must follow some change model or set of processes.

In my consulting I come across many professionals who are frustrated in their jobs because they see their organizations make the same mistakes over and over. There is nothing as debilitating as analyzing an experience (debriefing) to identify the solution to some underlying problem but then not taking the required action to put the solution into actual practice. Learning must be regarded as an intervention and handled in the same way as a change project— by using OD principles. There is a need for preparation, persistence, and follow-up.

Several years ago, while employed by a social services organization, I worked in the area of quality management. My responsibilities included conducting studies on customer satisfaction and organizational effectiveness. After every study was completed (reflection phase), we developed action plans based on the implications of our research. To help with the utilization and follow-up process, we developed a simple tracking device (Chart 5-1) to keep everyone informed of follow-up action that was deemed necessary (DiBella, 1990). As stages of follow-up were completed, we kept track of our progress using this device, which was periodically distributed to everyone with either implementation responsibilities or who was affected by the changes being put into place. This simple process of informing staff of what had actually been accomplished and what yet needed to be done kept the utilization process alive. It served as a constant reminder that the debriefing wasn't complete until the required action had been taken.

Chart 5-1
Debrief Tracking Report

Event	Date of Event	Date of Debrief	Actions Agreed Upon	Action Date	Responsible Agent	Action Status

4. Increase Frequency

Once your team or organization has an established and successful debriefing process, a good way to enhance learning is simply to increase the frequency of debriefings. Unfortunately, this is easier said than done since debriefing requires resources for learning and reflection—time, money, and personnel. Given the need for organizations to minimize costs, many managers make decisions about allocating resources only when they know a priori the return on that investment. Since the payoff from learning investments is uncertain or nonmonetary, it can be difficult to justify making learning expenditures. Learning is a difficult sell, but as the saying goes, "If you think learning is expensive, try ignorance."

The key to this challenge is finding ways to integrate debriefing activities into established ones. For example, if your workgroup has regular staff meetings, make debriefing a regular part of the agenda. Monthly or quarterly review meetings also provide a convenient and complementary venue for debriefing.

Some companies give special, periodic attention to learning events by establishing attention-getting programs like L.L. Bean's Mistake-of-the-Month club. Such programs must be fun and rewarding for employees (prizes for the best presentation of a mistake and lesson learned) and conducted infrequently enough so they do not interfere with meeting everyday work requirements. Qualcomm Corp. organizes Friday afternoon socials during which employees make presentations about lessons learned; Nortel Networks sponsors "lunch & learn" sessions to encourage staff to share their expertise. These sessions are optional, so they do not compete with the need for resources elsewhere.

Designing New *Learning Events*

Taking time out to debrief past experiences is an engaging, yet reactive form of learning. It is reactive in the sense that the organization learns only from events that have occurred. When such events lead to insight, "serendipitous learning" takes place. However, whether that learning conforms to the strategic direction of the firm or organization is a matter of chance.

A more strategic approach is to design learning events that intentionally create or represent the learning approaches in your desired learning profile. A colleague of mine, Steve Cabana, refers to these events as "learning containers." Events and experiences can be intentionally designed and orchestrated to produce insight that helps a team or organization work more effectively. We can refer to such initiatives as "experimental learning" and can shape them to conform to the characteristics of a team's desired profile. Following are three ways to do so:

- Identify Knowledge Needs or Learning Content
- Identify *Who* Needs to Know *What* and *When*
- Protect the Fragility of Experiments

1. Identify Knowledge Needs or Learning Content

The aim of "orchestrated learning" is to design situations that will produce knowledge beyond what a team or organization already has access to. In effect, we want to create knowledge that lies beyond existing boundaries or beyond one's knowledge space. To do so requires an awareness about what a team does and does not know. Figure 5-2 represents a simple schema I have used with clients to help them become aware of their knowledge gaps and learning needs.

The aim of "orchestrated learning" is to enlarge the domain of what is known and shared (block 1). Some knowledge already exists within the group but is not shared since it is either in tacit form or cannot be discussed because of cultural taboos (block 2). If that's the team problem, then learning experiments should be designed to affect how knowledge is retained (LOr 3) and disseminated (LOr 4).

When teams and organizations can identify what they don't know (block 3), learning experiments can be designed to address that knowledge shortcoming. Often this gap focuses on issues of process versus content (LOr 2), value creation (LOr 6), or innovation (LOr 5). The most critical domain is a team's blind side (block 4), or void, which pertains to knowledge shortcomings that the group itself is not aware of. This problem often suggests that a team or organization is too inwardly focused or myopic and needs to become more externally oriented (LOr 1).

2. Identify Who Needs to Know What and When

Some of the knowledge needed by a team or organization pertains to individual capabilities, and some relates to team or group capabilities (LOr 7). The latter is especially critical when there is a need for coor-

Figure 5-2
Knowledge Boundaries

	What is Discussed?	**What is Not Discussed?**
KNOWLEDGE WITHIN	Explicit, (1) Shared Knowledge	Tacit or (2) Undiscussible?
KNOWLEDGE OUTSIDE	Acknowledging (3) the Unknown	Void (4)

dinated action by a team. Learning events must relate to where the emphasis is needed.

Many firms have developed competency models to identify the set of skills needed to perform various occupational roles. Developing individual learning or training plans is one way in which companies specify who needs to know what. If a firm's current training regimen does not provide the required competencies, then new learning experiences must be designed to make up the difference. In some regulated industries, learning plans must conform to industry requirements and certification rules.

With the growing emphasis on workgroups and cross-functional workteams, many organizations are focusing on collective capabilities (group Learning Focus) and the synergies that can be obtained therefrom. Learning events that involve entire teams or workgroups can direct training toward these needs. A popular way to do so is through group experiential exercises such as ropes courses or Outward Bound–type programs. Teamwork on simulators and role-play games are other popular methods to promote group learning. As a way to get teams to focus on their collective needs, a colleague of mine, Marilyn Darling, works with clients to develop their "Team Learning Charter." This pact specifies what a team needs to know and identifies the actions that will promote that learning.

Finally, it is important to consider the issue of time: When is the learning needed? How soon will it be used? Given time pressures at most workplaces, this is no trivial matter. "Just-in-case learning" (just in case you may need it) is a luxury except for those professions (nuclear plant operations, aircraft piloting, medical practice, sea-and-land rescue) where unusual circumstances may mean life or death and inadequate training can lead to disaster. When time is of the essence, teams do not have recourse to external Knowledge Source (LOr 1), and public Knowledge Reserve (LOr 3) (instruction or procedures manuals) must be readily available.

A more efficient use of learning resources would emphasize "just-in-time learning," making the knowledge available when and where it will be put to use. Timeliness also relates to the quality of the learning in two ways. First, the more time that passes after something has been learned, the less accessible it becomes (forgetting curve). Second, the more time passes, the less valued or up-to-date is the knowledge that gets applied (knowledge depreciation curve). The key then is "learning punctuality," learning something when you need to know it, which is not about the speed of learning or the rapidity of learning events as much as their timeliness. The critical questions for a team then become: What does it need to know? and When does it need to know it? The answers are situational or context specific. However, with those considerations made, events or experiments can be designed accordingly.

3. Protect the Fragility of Experiments

When successful, learning events and experiments generate insights that redirect team or organizational activities or promote the dissemination of knowledge in new ways. Either way, they create results or produce strategic action that challenges an organization's culture or modus operandi. These outcomes become a source of conflict and friction between the new and old and are subject to conformity pressures.

For this reason, Herbert Shepard (1984) pointed out the need to design experiments to ensure their success. He suggested that change agents "build umbrellas" to protect the fragility of experiments. One way to do so is to establish shared ownership through voluntary staff involvement. Learning experiments should not be hidden from staff but given visibility and nurturing support. The need to protect learning initiatives from the inertia of large bureaucratic organizations can also be addressed through the creation of parallel learning structures (Bushe & Shani, 1991).

The preceding three issues (identifying knowledge needs, identifying who needs to know what when, and protecting experiments) represent parameters whereby learning experiences can be designed to fit organizational learning needs and demands. To ensure strategic learning events, their parameters must first be specified. Then learning events can be designed in conformity to and in alignment with desired LOrs and in this way can concurrently enhance multiple learning approaches.

Focusing on Singular Learning Orientations

Interventions that focus on singular Learning Orientations involve the enhancement or shift of specific learning approaches. There are some general guidelines for these types of intervention as well as idiosyncratic ones that pertain to each of the seven LOrs. As much as the LOrs are dissimilar (since each represents a different dimension of learning capability), they are similar in being derived from research on actual learning activities.

LOrs represent embedded processes that have been intentionally or latently created through patterns of social interaction in some organizational or collective setting. Changing learning approaches means fomenting a fundamental shift in underlying culture and patterns of interaction or communication. This challenge places the task clearly in the domain of an OD intervention, and learning architects and strategists need to follow some change-process model. For example, to follow the Lewin-Schein model of change (Schein, 1987), we must first create some tension and anxiety that the current learning approaches are no longer effective or appropriate given the team's strategic direction. One way to do so is to remove supports for existing processes while increasing rewards and resources for the new ones.

The key is to recognize that shifting Learning Orientations is an intervention and should be handled within some change-management framework. A principal reason for the failure of many learning organization initiatives is that they impose new learning-related behaviors onto a template of existing ones. Such initiatives overlook the presence of existing capabilities, and no preparation is made for the transition. In the change framework (present state → transition state → future state) of Beckhard and Harris (1987), current learning approaches collectively represent the present state, and desired learning approaches represent the future state. Creating the latter requires meeting the challenges of the transition state. As we aim to shift a singular LOr, we must be mindful of what we are changing from and whether the shift requires adding or replacing behaviors. Also our focus needs to encompass the systems ramifications of any shift in behavior or learning approach.

Table 5-1 describes a variety of activities and behaviors that promote specific Learning Orientations. This set is presented as a suggested rather than an exhaustive one. The appropriateness of using a particular behavior or action for a team or organization will depend on the specific characteristics and context of that unit. Some general comments and issues that relate to singular LOrs now follow.

LOr 1: Knowledge Source

A problem in many teams and organizations is that they either undervalue their own experience and expertise (low internal Knowledge Source), and hence overvalue the experiences of others, or undervalue the experiences of others and suffer from the "not-invented-here" syndrome. Action in this Learning Orientation can rectify these extreme values. Teams and organizations can open themselves up to the wider

Table 5-1

Activities That Are Consistent with Specific Learning Approaches

Learning Orientation	Approach	Activities
Knowledge Source	Internal	Reduce outsourcing of work elements (functions, technical tasks)
		Re-establish internal functions that were previously given over to external suppliers
		Cut back on all forms of consulting and contracting
		Increase support for research
		Initiate a reward program for employee ideas and suggestions that positively affect net revenue
		Prepare a resource and capability directory that lists all employees by their areas of training and expertise
	External	Conduct benchmarking activities to compare your team or organization with others, either in the same or different industries
		Enroll your firm or its personnel in professional or trade associations
		Subscribe to industry information sources
		Form joint ventures or alliances with competitors, suppliers, or customers
		Increase staff participation in professional conferences
		Contract out for selected activities or functions that have historically been performed internally
		Reduce the influence of mindguards who buffer your team or organization from external sources of influence and increase support for information explorers
Content–Process Focus	Content	Define and develop projects on the basis of desired results and outcomes
		Conduct panel or focus groups to better identify what customers want or need

Table 5-1 (continued)
Activities That Are Consistent with Specific Learning Approaches

Learning Orientation	Approach	Activities
		Divide complex and lengthy activities into small phases with identifiable milestones
		Conduct product- or market-mapping exercises by identifying product attributes and how they map onto customer needs
	Process	Initiate business-process reengineering
		Create periodic opportunities for systems retooling or updating
		Reward staff who identify sources of process improvement
		Conduct formative evaluation studies on projects underway
Knowledge Reserve	Personal	Promote staff on the basis of what they know
		Make every effort to retain experienced workers
		Give staff sabbatical time to reflect on their experiences
		Encourage staff to create personal learning diaries
		Acknowledge employees who develop unique competencies
	Public	Integrate lessons from experience into routine procedures
		Maintain procedure manuals in domains where knowledge is explicit
		Conduct cultural events or fairs that reflect or exhibit corporate capabilities
		Locate bulletin boards or TV monitors throughout company facilities to broadcast company news
		Create electronic bulletin boards to post information on-line

Learning Orientation	Approach	Activities
		Sponsor a series of learning histories to capture and aggregate experience
Dissemination Mode	Formal	Create a corporate university and give it visibility
		Require staff to attend a certain number of training courses per year
		Design an extensive orientation program for all new staff
		Require staff to attend regular staff meetings
		Establish a policy that staff must access procedures manuals for authorized work processes or routines
		Require personnel who are approaching retirement to give seminars or workshops in their areas of expertise
	Informal	Create opportunities (time and space) for staff to mingle through better office design or during periods of recess
		Organize and invite staff to weekly Friday afternoon wine and cheese parties
		Provide resources for staff to participate in company retreats or periodic in-company conferences and annual awards meetings
		Require all staff to have acknowledged mentors and reward mentors for the contributions of their apprentices
		Develop apprenticeship programs and encourage all staff to participate
		Encourage the development of communities-of-practice
Learning Scope	Incremental	Identify job skills that contribute to product value and design employee training programs around those specific requirements

Table 5-1 (continued)
Activities That Are Consistent with Specific Learning Approaches

Learning Orientation	Approach	Activities
		Investigate the feasibility of meeting international standards or of being I.S.O. certified
		Establish continuous improvement processes
		Identify your sources of value creation
		Develop procedures for the regular debriefing of operating experience
	Transformative	Acknowledge the need to take risks in new ventures
		Don't penalize employees for innovative ventures that fail
		Support exercises (such as brainstorming, dialogue, and scenario planning) that challenge, set aside, or circumvent current thinking
		Provide rewards or new role models for alternative ways of working
		Establish product and process incubators and provide them with support outside of line operations and responsibilities
Value– Chain Focus	Design-Make	Develop joint ventures with organizations that have strong research and development capability
		Require marketing staff to rotate into temporary assignments in manufacturing and product development
		Develop proprietary knowledge about product design and manufacturing processes
		Increase spending for research and development
		Promote staff on the basis of their knowledge about production processes
	Market-Deliver	Develop joint ventures with organizations that have strong marketing capability

Table 5-1 (continued)
Activities That Are Consistent with Specific Learning Approaches

Learning Orientation	Approach	Activities
		Increase support for marketing research activities such as panel or focus-group discussions among customers
		Require all technical (engineering, production) staff to rotate into temporary assignments in marketing
		Use call centers to open up lines of communication with customers rather than just for product promotion or order taking
		Enhance product distribution channels
Learning Focus	Individual	Require staff to have personalized training and learning plans
		Allocate a set percentage of the operating budget or gross revenues to employee development programs
		Give staff time to pursue their own personal development
		Establish resource centers where employees can get educational support and guidance
	Group	Select employees on the basis of their ability to collaborate and work with others
		Build simulators or design simulated exercises to train intact teams or workgroups
		Send teams of employees rather than individuals to conferences and personal development seminars
		Include courses on teamwork and group process in training programs
		Provide bonuses to teams rather than, or in addition to, rewards given directly to individuals

world (external Knowledge Source) and take a more appreciative view of what's around them.

Knowledge Source really has to do with one's mental model of the relevant world. In effect, it pertains to whose knowledge has meaning to us and how boundaries, real or contrived, shape a team's or organization's socially constructed view of useful knowledge. To shift along the dimension of Knowledge Source requires a shift in identification and appreciation for the experiences of others.

The emergence of computerized information and communications technology has increased the permeability of organizational boundaries. This development has created opportunities for knowledge acquisition and sharing through the use of e-mail and the Internet. Teleconferencing and videoconferencing have created new learning venues of external Knowledge Source that span teams and organizations. Distance learning, Web-based learning, and virtual corporate universities are just three novel learning approaches that use these new technologies.

Another practice used by companies to expand their Knowledge Source is to participate in corporate consortiums (Botkin, 1999). Some such organizations are composed of intra-industry members, others represent multiple industries. For example, InterClass is an association of firms from diverse industries that collaborate to support learning about general business issues. The Marketing Science Institute is a collaboration among firms that supports collective learning specifically targeted on marketing functions and issues. Company representatives meet intermittently to share experiences or to support mutual learning experiments and thus provide new sources of knowledge.

LOr 2: Content–Process Focus

In recent years the corporate world has become increasingly more results oriented. Emphasis is placed on realizing specific outcomes and on monitoring and measuring performance, as evidenced by the popularity of such mechanisms as the "balanced scorecard" (Kaplan, 1992). In response, both consultants and clients are now more focused on the outcomes and effects of interventions and on using them as criteria by which consultant work is evaluated or compensated.

A major ramification of this shift has been a decreasing interest in process issues. This shift is consistent with a cultural orientation toward action rather than reflection and with a managerial trend to emphasize decentralized forms of management and enabling mechanisms such as empowerment. Managers don't want to be bothered with how-tos and are willing to give that responsibility to others; they just want to see results.

Although process engineering has garnered some attention, learning investments today are more often oriented toward products or outcomes. Even TQM programs, which have as a component continuous process improvement, place greater emphasis on designing and delivering products and services that meet customer needs. Teams and organizations in industries that have historically been sheltered from the marketplace, such as public utilities, are apt to be manufacturing or engineering oriented. However, changes in the world's economy have required even these firms to become more market driven. Where this has created performance pressure for firms, there needs to be a learning emphasis on product or outcome issues. A shift along Content–Process Focus can be expedited by recognizing the benefits derived from either approach.

LOr 3: Knowledge Reserve

As the world's developed economies transition from product to service industries, there has been a growing interest in the storage and accessibility of knowledge. Knowledge work and knowledge management are now popular management themes and initiatives. Computerized information technology has provided new and inexpensive ways to store certain forms of data and explicit knowledge and thus has increased the potential for public Knowledge Reserve. As the computer industry develops more hardware and software tools for database management and data mining, activities and methods for public Knowledge Reserve will grow even further.

Shifting from personal to public Knowledge Reserve can be accelerated by using these forms of computer technology. However, it also requires that experts be willing to place their knowledge in public forums, an act that is too often undermined where knowledge is treated as a unique source of power and authority. Personal Knowledge Reserve is also regarded as a source of status and employment security. To promote a shift along this Learning Orientation requires forms of reinforcement and rewards that reduce the expert's insecurity and sense of loss when tacit or privately held knowledge becomes explicit or public. Some teams and organizations may want to shift toward private Knowledge Reserve by ensuring proprietary ownership of knowledge that had previously been held in public. One way to make that shift is to develop the creativity and unique skills of individual workers.

LOr 4: Dissemination Mode

If it is true as suggested by research conducted by the Institute for Research on Learning that all learning is social, then there is already a great deal of informal learning taking place in most work settings (Wenger, 1998). However, this learning approach can be further encouraged by giving employees the time and space that increases the likelihood of informal sharing. That might include longer lunch breaks, more office parties or end-of-the-week socials, or larger hallways and common areas where employees can congregate serendipitously. Shifting from informal to formal dissemination means increasing or giving greater visibility to various forms of organized learning activities such as event debriefing, worker training or orientation programs, or career development programs.

To balance both formal and informal Dissemination Mode, it is important to address the need for collective and private space in office environments. Furniture manufacturers, like Steelcase, have focused on this need by designing and marketing office furniture and equipment that encourages employee interaction. Other companies, like Apple Computer, have configured entire building layouts with office design to combine private and common space (Markoff, 1993).

LOr 5: Learning Scope

Learning Scope pertains to our frame of reference regarding the application of knowledge and whether we are aiming to improve existing products or ways of working or to create entirely new ones. This Learning Orientation represents the relative investment that teams make in correction as opposed to innovation. Shifting from incremental to transformative Learning Scope requires an ability to look at the world from a different framework or set of assumptions. Exercises and games such as brainstorming, playing devil's advocate, suspending judgement of thought, using the practice of dialogue, or asking what-if questions can move teams to think in new ways or to open up their thinking horizon.

Fundamentally, the shift along the incremental–transformative axis pertains to changes in risk taking. If we focus learning investments on incremental issues, we seek to answer questions or solve problems that have immediate relevance. The results of incremental learning are minimally disruptive since they mean doing more of what we already do or doing it better. When we seek to learn within new paradigms, we can never be sure what the payoff might be, and we risk learning about domains of knowledge that ultimately challenge or disrupt what we already do. To move between these learning approaches means altering a team's or organization's acceptance of risk.

LOr 6: Value–Chain Focus

Value–Chain Focus (design-make–market-deliver) represents the line of continuity that stretches from the conceptualization of a product and service to its delivery to the customer. As a product or service moves through this line, its value is shaped by professionals in different functional domains. Indeed, many firms are still structured by functional expertise (marketing, finance, engineering, etc.), and the focus of most workers stems primarily from their professional affiliation and identity. Teams and companies are often oriented toward a particular function perhaps because of the profession of their founder or CEO. Shifting along the design-make–market-deliver axis means altering functional emphasis between engineering and marketing.

LOr 7: Learning Focus

In contemporary American management literature, much attention is placed on the benefits of teams and how new communication and information technologies can expedite teamwork. The growing demand for teamwork suggests a shift toward promoting the learning of teams and groups versus the development of individuals. The difficulty in making this shift is that most of the developed nations of the world have cultures that value individualism over collectivism (Hofstede, 1991). In those organizational contexts where the desire to shift learning investments is consistent with the dominant societal culture, the change is apt to be supported. The challenge arises where the shift is countercultural (i.e., toward investing in group learning activities in individualistic cultures and individual learning in collectivist ones).

To increase support for team learning in individualistic cultures, a change agent needs to highlight those work domains or performance pressures where coordination among employees is a prerequisite to a successful project. Where teamwork is valued and there is a desire to shift to more individual-focused learning, a change agent needs to point out that the capability of teams is dependent in part on individual competence. Overreliance on one form of learning or another limits the development of overall capability.

This chapter has covered ways in which teams and organizations can enhance or shift their Learning Orientations. Now we turn to those factors that can improve the nature of what gets learned or accelerate how that learning occurs.

Learning Practices: Lesson 5

The return on learning investments is greater where there is a shared recognition of its value. Use time and space in creative ways to build shared reflective processes. Support diverse practices to strengthen Learning Orientations.

6

Promoting the Conditions
for Learning

> *Learning is not attained by chance. It must be sought for*
> *with ardor and attended to with diligence.*
> —Abigail Adams

One key workplace resource that is perceived to be in increasingly short supply is time. Companies don't have time to invest in learning, and when they do, they want to speed up the learning process. Some forms of learning are like rocking chairs—you can speed up the process, but you still won't get anywhere. Then there are styles of learning that are like baking bread—you can turn up the heat, but all you'll do is burn the bread.

In this chapter we look at ways to enhance the effectiveness of learning by strengthening the Facilitating Factors. Learning Orientations determine the style of a team's learning. However, it's the FFs that make that style effective or that expedite its realization by promoting the conditions that allow learning to occur. My research and client work have indicated that together these 10 Facilitating Factors create a powerful context that is supportive of learning. When that context is in place, learning is more apt to occur and to occur more rapidly.

Scenarios for Selecting Interventions That Strengthen Facilitating Factors

Teams and organizations that want to make their learning style more effective or rapid can do so by strengthening specific Facilitating Factors that support learning in any setting. There are many practices,

Figure 6-1
Scale of Intervention to Promote Facilitating Factors

		Weak	Strong
FELT NEED	**Strong**	3. Focused	4. Assault
	Weak	1. Prepare	2. Focused

Weak   **Strong**

RESOURCES

processes, and actions that can help teams and organizations learn. However, successful action requires a readiness to act, a commitment to learning, as well as the availability of resources that can be applied to make learning investments.

A team's desired learning profile presumably identifies areas where it has a felt need to improve, but its actual readiness to do so does not necessarily follow from this, cannot be assured nor can the resources needed to undertake any action always be relied upon. Whether one focuses on a singular FF or on multiple FFs as the point of intervention depends on the organization's state of readiness and the amount of resources it has available. Figure 6-1 shows the four possible scenarios that organizations face as they consider ways to enhance FFs.

The four scenarios represented in Figure 6-1 are best addressed through one of three intervention strategies. When an organization lacks the resources to promote learning and there is little felt need (cell 1), it is best to engage the organization in preparation rather than action. It makes little sense to initiate an intervention when there is little receptivity. If either "felt need" or "resources" is weak (cells 2 and 3), then an intervention that focuses on a singular FF is preferred. If both "felt need" and "resources" are strong (cell 4), then a systemic effort to promote several FFs is appropriate. These three general strategies are further described below.

Intervention Strategies

There are three general strategies to accelerate learning by promoting the conditions that foster it:

- Prepare through recognition of a concern, need, or underlying problem (scenario 1)
- Focus on one or two specific Facilitating Factors (scenarios 2 and 3)
- Make an all-out assault (scenario 4)

1. Prepare Through Recognition of a Concern, Need, or Underlying Problem

When both "felt need" and "resources" are weak, an organization faces some significant barriers to learning. The magnitude of these barriers varies from one team to another; hence the leverage points to enhance learning will similarly vary. Consequently, there is no one best way to promote the conditions that foster learning. Change agents need to use a team's own self-critique as a driving force for learning. When there is shared agreement about what a team needs to learn or about barriers to its learning, it's possible to take action that will have positive long-term implications. This occurs when a team's actions create a context for learning and thereby address underlying problems rather than superficial symptoms.

Rather than start with one or more FFs in order to create such a learning environment de novo, it is better to prepare a team to work on FFs by making the connection with an existing felt need (or dissatisfaction) or shared concern. The ability of team members to themselves identify the problems that restrain their learning is a propelling force for change. When we acknowledge and make use of the energy of that force, we are less apt to meet resistance. Thus it is better to start with existing problems or concerns as they are presently perceived and then to determine which of the 10 FFs can be most helpful in resolving them. In this fashion we aren't imposing some prescriptive model but are starting with the context that is, before actually working on FFs.

One way to define learning challenges is to review the desired learning profile and identify which Learning Orientations the team

Table 6-1
Guide for Developing Learning Orientations

To Develop Capability in These Approaches			Focus on These Facilitating Factors
LOr 1	Knowledge Source	Internal	Organizational Curiosity Concern for Measurement Performance Gap
		External	Systems Perspective Continuous Education Operational Variety Scanning Imperative
LOr 2	Content–Process Focus	Content	Concern for Measurement
		Process	Operational Variety
LOr 3	Knowledge Reserve	Personal	Involved Leadership Multiple Advocates
		Public	Climate of Openness Continous Education
LOr 4	Dissemination Mode	Formal	Climate of Openness
		Informal	Organizational Curiosity
LOr 5	Learning Scope	Incremental	Performance Gap Concern for Measurement
		Transformative	Organizational Curiosity Scanning Imperative Systems Perspective

Table 6-1 *(Continued)*
Guide for Developing Learning Orientations

To Develop Capability in These Approaches		Focus on These Facilitating Factors
LOr 6 Value–Chain Focus	Design-Make	Operational Variety Organizational Curiosity
	Market-Deliver	Scanning Imperative
LOr 7 Learning Focus	Individual	Involved Leadership Continuous Education
	Group	Multiple Advocates Systems Perspective

feels it needs to change. My research and work with clients have indicated that the process of changing learning approaches can be enhanced if work is done on specific FFs. Table 6-1 exhibits relationships between LOrs and FFs and provides guidance on what teams could focus on. For example, if a team feels that its greatest need is to improve internal Knowledge Source, then it should develop its capability in Organizational Curiosity, Concern for Measurement, or Performance Gap.

The key is to build on a felt need for change and then take advantage of a team's energy and interest in addressing that problem area or need. The felt need for change is a critical factor in galvanizing interest and commitment. An overt desire to shift learning approaches signals a felt need for change and points toward specific FFs to promote such approaches.

2. Focus on One or Two Specific Facilitating Factors

Once a decision is made to focus on specific FFs, actions can be taken to enhance a team's capability in those factors. Table 6-2 is an inventory of learning practices describing a range of actions, practices, and behaviors that support the FFs. If a desired profile reveals a need to change one or several FFs, Table 6-2 can be used to identify corresponding actions to address that need.

Table 6-2
Activities That Are Consistent with Specific Facilitating Factors

Facilitating Factors	Activities, Behaviors
Scanning Imperative	Monitor news reports for information that relates to your firm's products and services
	Increase funds for employees to attend industry and professional conferences
	Subscribe to professional research journals and monitor their contents for developments in technology, customer interests, and market conditions
	Visit customers and suppliers
	Identify types of external events that can be analyzed as learning opportunities
Performance Gap	Raise expectations about performance
	Benchmark your team's activities and performance against world-class competitors
	Disseminate information about the performance of your firm's chief competitors
	Engage staff in developing a shared vision of long-term success
	Identify shortcomings in individual and team behavior
Concern for Measurement	Conduct seminars in new forms of accounting such as the "balanced scorcard" (Kaplan, 1992)
	Use bulletin and poster boards to place information on performance indicators throughout publicly accessible buildings and facilities
	Discuss performance measures during regular staff meetings
	Incorporate indicators in all production and performance plans

Table 6-2 *(Continued)*
Activities That Are Consistent with Specific Facilitating Factors

Facilitating Factors	Activities, Behaviors
Organizational Curiosity	Institutionalize brainstorming as a team exercise
	Train staff in scenario planning (Van der Heijden, 1996)
	Encourage what-if thinking
	Place toys and mind-teasing games in meeting rooms and other publicly accessible places
	Give prizes for the most outrageous ideas about new products or process technologies
Climate of Openness	Train staff in the principles of dialogue (Isaacs, 1999)
	Don't "kill the messenger"
	Use two-column exercises to surface unarticulated conflict (Senge, 1990)
	Promote a "no retribution" policy for nonconformist beliefs and activities that do not jeopardize the team or company mission
	Use open space activities to set meeting agendas (Owen, 1997)
	Promote the principles of open-book management (Case, 1995)
Continuous Education	Allocate a set percentage or amount of funds for training and other learning activities
	Require all staff to have personal development plans
	Make mentoring a required responsibility of all managerial staff
	Provide resources to promote on-line, asynchronous, virtual learning
	Provide time and space for staff to socialize informally

Table 6-2 *(Continued)*
Activities That Are Consistent with Specific Facilitating Factors

Facilitating Factors	Activities, Behaviors
Operational Variety	Focus workgroup productivity on outcomes, not on how tasks are be accomplished
	Have human resource policies (in benefits, work schedules) that accommodate different staff needs
	Form workgroups and task forces with employees from different backgrounds
	Maintain multiple work processes that operate in parallel
	Have competency models that allow variance in behaviors
Multiple Advocates	Promote the role of devil's advocate in staff meetings
	Allow several staff members to attend the same professional development conferences
	Encourage staff to work in partnership with others on change initiatives
	Use debate teams to argue different points of view on some pending issue or decision
	Give implementation responsibilities to teams rather than to individuals
Involved Leadership	Promote managers on their ability to coach and develop staff
	Require managers to oversee periodic debriefing sessions
	Encourage managers to lead professional development seminars
	Make operational activities into learning activities to emphasize learning through action
	Promote only managers who exhibit support for learning activities in their behavior and through their decisions

Table 6-2 *(Continued)*
Activities That Are Consistent with Specific Facilitating Factors

Facilitating Factors	Activities, Behaviors
Systems Perspective	Analyze situations, problems, and olutions in terms of their long-term implications
	Solicit perspectives on courses of action from differing parts of the organization
	Establish a system of job rotation as part of an employee's personal development
	Hire staff on the basis of their employ-ment experience in different parts of the organization
	Sponsor training programs and courses in systems dynamics and systems think-ing tools

Table 6-2 is not an exhaustive list of actions that promote learn-ing. It is presented here merely to suggest that there are numerous ways to do so. While the notion of "best practices" has come into vogue, it is dangerous to think that what may be best for some is best for all. (In Chapter 9, we will explore the parameters of using "best practices.") Practitioners and change agents must use discretion in selecting specific actions to build the learning context for their organizations.

3. Make an All-Out Assault

Analyses of learning profile data have indicated that there are syner-gistic effects among the Facilitating Factors. As a team develops pro-ficiency in one FF, it is more likely to develop capability in other FFs. Thus it is more effective to work on many Facilitating Factors at once than on one or two at a time. This strategy, however, is successful only when an organization has the necessary resources and the felt need for change is strong.

The aim of an "all-out assault" approach is to rapidly shape a context that promotes learning. The resultant comprehensive and intensive intervention can be threatening to team or organizational members; thus, for this strategy to succeed, the felt need must be strong. Where it is not in evidence, a more incremental—FF by FF—and less threatening strategy is advised.

Action Planning

Whichever strategy is ultimately adopted, a team must come up with a plan to implement it. One way to ensure implementation is to develop a written action plan that can be shared among team members. Chart 6-1 contains the format for an action plan that is based on a strategy of focused intervention and is grounded in problem identification. Both FFs and LOrs are listed since they may both be part of an intervention.

Chart 6-2 is an action plan completed by a client I have worked with. Note the connection back to the learning profile and how actions are focused on both FFs and LOrs.

In this chapter we covered some generic and specific strategies and actions to create the context for learning. Both shifting learning approaches and creating the context for learning are systems interventions and forms of organization development. Despite an abundance of models of change intervention, there are no set formulas on change that work for all settings. However, as we have in this chapter, we can identify various actions and behaviors that promote learning and change. The overlooked challenge is adapting actions and behaviors to specific contexts and to that we now turn in Chapter 7.

Learning Practices: Lesson 6

Learning requires resources combined with focused action and commitment. Build a commitment to learning by addressing felt needs or critical problems. Engage in learning practices that relate to shared needs.

Chart 6-1
Action Plan Format

Improve Learning Capability Based on a Critical Problem, Challenge, or
Opportunity Facing the Team or Organization

Action Plan
Team or organization profiled: _____
Team members: _____
Date: _____

Steps of the Action Plan
1. Problem Identification
Describe an important problem, challenge, or opportunity currently facing
your team that can be resolved by developing learning capability:

_____
_____
_____
_____
_____
_____
_____

2. Learning Profile Revisited
Looking back at your learning profile form, which Facilitating Factors
and/or Learning Orientations will be helpful in resolving your problem?

Orientations: _____

Facilitating Factors: _____

3. Specific Changes
Using the Orientations and Factors as guides, describe what you will change
(behaviors, policies, processes) in order to resolve the problem or challenge:

_____
_____
_____
_____
_____
_____
_____
_____

Chart 5-1
Continued

___

4. Actions
What actions will you take to resolve the problem?

_____

_____

_____

_____

_____

_____

_____

_____

_____

5. What is your expected timeframe?

_____

_____

6. How will you measure the success of your actions?

_____

_____

_____

_____

_____

_____

_____

Chart 6-2
Action Plan Example

Improve Learning Capability Based on a Critical Problem, Challenge, or Opportunity Facing the Team or Organization

The following action plan is an example of an engineering group trying to take action in a changing environment. The group is converting to a new computer system that will have a significant effect on the way the group tracks its product development process and shares information with the rest of the organization.

Action Plan

Team or organization profiled: Engineering Group, Hitech, Inc.

Team members: Jose Perez, John Philipps, Susan Wong, Abigail Zy

Date: 12/00/00

Steps of the Action Plan

1. Problem Identification
Describe an important problem, challenge, or opportunity currently facing your team that can be resolved by developing learning capability:

Our engineering group has been told that we need to introduce a new computer system to improve the development of our hardware and software products. Once it is in place, job functions will change. All of our development processes from conception through design to marketing will be tracked on the new system. Product designs will be available on the network for all to see and criticize. Some of our customers will have early access to designs and be able to suggest engineering changes online long before the final product exists.

2. Learning Profile Revisited
Looking back at your learning profile form, which Facilitating Factors and/or Learning Orientations will be helpful in resolving your problem?

Orientations: *Dissemination Mode, Learning Focus*
Facilitating Factors: *Involved Leadership, Systems Perspective*

3. Specific Changes
Using the Orientations and Factors as guides, describe what you will change (behaviors, policies, processes) in order to resolve the problem or challenge:

Chart 5-2
Continued

Dissemination Mode—*We need to move from informal sharing of information. As we change computer systems, we all need to have some formal training.*

Learning Focus—*We need to move from reliance on individual learning to team learning in order to make this a successful transition.*

Involved Leadership—*We need Bob, our manager, to be actively involved in working with us to learn about the new system. Susan should be working closely with him and guiding all of us since she knows more about the system than anyone.*

Systems Perspective—*The new computer systems will affect the way the design group submits and approves its designs and the way our customers interact with us, so we need to engage them in the change process to make a smooth transition.*

4. Actions
What actions will you take to resolve the problem?
The first step will be a meeting with the entire engineering group, the design group, and some customers (systems perspective). Bob and Susan should lead the meeting to inform everyone about the expected changes resulting from the new computer systems (involved leadership). Susan will design some ongoing training sessions on the new computer (learning focus). These sessions will be videotaped for anyone else who would like to participate but can't make the sessions (dissemination mode). Mary, one of the engineers, is an expert on team learning. We will invite her to help us in working to be more effective team learners (learning focus).

5. What is your expected timeframe?
The meeting with Bob and Susan will happen in early February. The educational sessions will be designed and will begin in early March. Susan has volunteered to contact Mary about team learning.

6. How will you measure the success of your actions?
Early success will be measured by our actually doing what is in the timeframe listed above. Future success will be measured by how quickly everyone learns the new computer system and how that affects the quality of our work. We will develop a customer feedback survey to see how the change has affected them.

7

Learning Across Team and Corporate Boundaries

A truth on one side of the Pyrenees
is a falsehood on the other.
— Descartes

Promoting Learning in a Multi-Team Environment

The previous two chapters presented ideas and described practices to promote learning within a specific team or organization. In this chapter we will consider the special circumstances that exist when working within the context of multiple teams or organizations. The more complex an organization, as reflected in its functional and geographical breadth, the greater the challenge and the greater the opportunities and benefits to be gained from cross-organizational learning.

In a multi-team environment, or within an organization or firm that has multiple functional areas and work domains, practitioners face two possible learning scenarios. The first involves sharing information and integrating experiences across different teams to produce new knowledge. The second occurs when companies take existing ideas and practices that are used in one setting (team, department, functional area) and attempt to duplicate them in another setting. In the first scenario a set of teams or social units collectively invests in learning, doing so under the belief that in order to generate knowledge and produce new solutions, it is better to work in coordination rather than in isolation. The expected result is the creation of new knowledge and shared learning. In the second scenario, one team learns what another team has already discovered or developed.

A key process in promoting learning across different teams is communication. The development and accessibility of communications technology has simplified and accelerated the dissemination of knowledge and the ease with which people can converse with one another. Some recent communications developments come from new material products such as telephones, fax machines, and computerized electronic networks. Others come from process techniques such as open space, future search, and dialogue. Computer software products that support distance- and Web-based learning and cross-team collaboration have effectively reduced the constraints of physical separation. Information technology products provide the virtual working space that allows teams to post, store, retrieve, and share ideas and conversations that produce knowledge.

The challenge in promoting learning in a multi-team environment does not derive from a lack of dissemination tools or from the permeability of workgroup boundaries. With new communications and information-processing technology, work space boundaries are becoming more and more permeable, if not transparent. The critical issue is the extent to which different teams can identify with one another and can promote synergy rather than conflict from team differences. Otherwise, it's possible to create a situation whereby one team's solution becomes another team's problem!

Social Boundaries and the Divergence of Learning Styles

As Ed Schein (1992, 1999b) has pointed out in his work on organizational culture, companies are composed of different subcultures. These subcultures arise, in part, from the diverse challenges and experiences that separate teams must face and resolve. When we move between companies, cultural differences are magnified. One of the implications is differing perceptions between teams and organizations of the same phenomenon. Consequently, the perceived meaning, value, and use of a learning practice will vary between teams and workgroups in the same or in a different company.

Cultural variation is reflected in the different ways that teams learn and process information and knowledge. In using the *Organizational Learning Inventory* in client workshops, I have collected "learning profiles" of a variety of teams and functional groups. These data show that the learning approaches of, for example, marketing teams differ from the learning approaches of teams of engineers. Similar differences in learning approaches can be seen in other contrasting teams. When one team learns differently from the way another learns, it is not surprising that knowledge is rarely transferred between them, or that when it is transferred, such knowledge is rarely used.

Consider the learning profiles depicted in Figure 7-1 taken from a company that designs, manufactures, and sells computer chips. In Figure 7-1 "A" represents the profile data from a manufacturing engineer group in that firm, while "B" represents the profile of a team of product managers.

There are two principal points of difference between these two teams: the type of knowledge they value (LOr 2, LOr 6) and the ways in which they perceive their repositories of knowledge (LOr 1, LOr 3). Quite naturally, the engineering group is oriented toward knowledge of process and design, while the marketing team values knowledge about products and services and their delivery. When it comes to locating valued knowledge, the engineering group relies on its own internal and personal sources, while the marketing team focuses on external and public sources.

Figure 7-1
Organizational Learning Profile Data for Two Workteams (A, B)

LEARNING ORIENTATIONS:

		Mostly	More	Even	More	Mostly	
1. Knowledge Source	Internal		A		B		External
2. Content– Process Focus	Content	B			A		Process
3. Knowledge Reserve	Personal	A		B			Public
4. Dissemination Mode	Formal		B	A			Informal
5. Learning Scope	Incremental		A	B			Trans- formative
6. Value–Chain Focus	Design- Make	A			B		Market- Deliver
7. Learning Focus	Individual		AB				Group

Key: **A** = Team of Manufacturing Engineers
   B = Team of Product Managers

The learning approaches of these two groups could be viewed as complementary. However, their differences can be problematic if not recognized or if not processed well. For example, if these two teams were to collaborate on a learning task, they might soon realize that what knowledge they would consider and where they would go for that knowledge would differ. Unless each team appreciated those differences, they would become sources of frustration.

Yet the need to bring together teams from different functional areas is critical given the complexity of today's business problems and the need to develop integrated solutions. One way that businesses are trying to reduce cycle times in new-product development, for example, is through simultaneous or concurrent engineering. This form of work design shifts problem solving from a set of linear, sequential tasks to one in which teams from different functional areas (product engineers, manufacturing engineers, product managers) work together on the same project or problem. Their different learning approaches can generate problem solutions that could not be realized if such teams were working in isolation.

Promoting Learning in the Context of Multiple Teams

When teams try to learn from one another or work together to learn collaboratively, they will inevitably confront the challenge of distinctive learning profiles. The key to a harmonious integration of their differences is to first identify them and make them manifest. Creating organizational learning profile data opens a window to recognize and understand differences in learning approaches. Points of difference can serve to focus engagement and discussion between different teams or workgroups.

When I facilitate workshops among corporate teams and functions to create their learning profiles, I prompt discussion by asking team members to comment on any points of comparison (similarities or differences) between profile data. If this does not provoke discussion or dialogue, I then pose a set of questions to further help the process along. Some of the questions I pose are as follows:

- Where do the differences come from?
- How do the differences explain problems that may have existed in the relations between teams?
- In what ways do the differences create possibilities for collaborative learning between teams?

- Do any differences in learning approaches have to be reduced in order for diverse teams to learn collaboratively?
- If so, which ones, and how will those changes be made?

The aim of such conversations is to get team members to reflect on the significance and implications of team differences. The principle at work is that through conversation team members learn and create their own shared meaning. They also perform their own diagnosis, which can be a form of dialogue and change. When such conversations are held jointly among diverse teams, shared meaning can lead to shared action.

Learning "Best Practices" Between Teams or Across Boundaries of Cultural Difference

A second learning scenario takes place when one team (which I will refer to as the recipient) tries to learn from the experiences or developed practice of another team (which I will refer to as the originator). Learning across teams and other boundaries of cultural difference occurs when companies take a particular competence or process that exists within one team (originator) and use it in another (recipient). For example, when a global firm's marketing team in England develops a successful advertising campaign, there can be a concerted effort to transfer that campaign to other markets. Similarly, a human resource technique, such as incentive pay, that motivates employees in one part of a firm can be used to motivate employees in another part.

While learning advocates promote the dissemination of learning "best practices," the realities and complexities of different team and organizational cultures create significant problems for their implementation. First, the perceived meaning and value of a learning practice will vary between teams and workgroups. Second, the cultural assumptions and the dynamics that make the practice successful in the originating team may not be valid in the recipient team. The challenges of successfully sharing "best practices" can be seen in the following example.

A number of years ago a close friend of mine, Zack Taylor, who was a Peace Corps volunteer in Africa, told me the following story. Zack had been assigned as an agricultural extension agent to help peasant farmers in a small village use new soil-tilling practices to increase crop yields. The practices had been introduced several years earlier by another Peace Corps volunteer, named Peter, who had written in his exit report that the initiative had been very successful. While Peter was in the village over the duration of two harvests, the new tilling practices had led to a small increase in crop yield the first year and a larger one during the second.

My friend's assignment was to build on the work of his predecessor by introducing new crop varieties whose proliferation would be enhanced by the new tilling practices. However, when Zack arrived, he discovered that all the farmers were using their traditional forms of tilling rather than those introduced by the previous Peace Corps volunteer. When Zack inquired about why they had stopped using the new tilling practices, he was told that they had "belonged" to Peter and since he was no longer in the village, they had returned to their own ways of tilling the soil.

The message in this story is that to disseminate and try out "best practices" is one thing, to institutionalize them is another. The latter is not apt to occur when the recipients cannot identify with or develop a sense of ownership toward the new practice. As long as the originator or owner of the innovative or best practice is present or known, it has meaning, but when value is not developed within the recipient or target group, the probability of sustaining the practice is low. The dilemma faced by my friend in the Peace Corps is not unlike the experience of many organizations that build repositories of "best practices" and aim to have those practices disseminated across workgroup boundaries. This learning process breaks down when the time comes to institutionalize or legitimate the practice into on-going action.

For "best practices" to take hold in a recipient system, the participants in that system must develop some empathy with or appreciation for the originators of the practice or develop their own identification with it. When managers borrow or emulate "best practices" developed elsewhere, their chance of realizing successful outcomes depends on their ability to create user identification with the emulated practice. Managers who impose a "best practice" or require that it be replicated without alteration prevent new users from developing a sense of ownership, and the result is often disappointing. The way for managers to promote utilization is to facilitate a process of adaptation that builds identification, meaning, and value for the recipient group. Such an approach allows the practice to be reshaped to fit the nuances and particular attributes of the recipient system. What makes practices "best" is their effectiveness; what makes practices effective is that they promote action and constructive change; what produces action within a team is its sense of ownership and identification with the practice.

While whole societies, as in the preceding Peace Corps example, learn (or try to learn) practices from one another, work organizations also engage in this activity. For example, during the past ten years "Six Sigma" has become increasingly appreciated and visible as a "best practice" to increase organizational effectiveness. This practice—really a set of practices—was first developed and named by Motorola as a strategy to improve product and manufacturing quality. It has since been diffused into other large corporate giants such as General Electric. To help managers and companies learn "Six Sigma," Motorola's corporate university conducted courses that were open to outside organizations. GE employees were among the first to participate. While they learned the principles of "Six Sigma" at Motorola University, their subsequent challenge was to adapt them to the particular work demands and conditions at GE.

A Model of Practice Diffusion and Adaptation

In examining how organizations diffuse new practices, Zaltman et al. (1984) developed a two-staged process model. Zaltman (1984, p. 10) was particularly concerned with the diffusion of innovation—any idea, practice, or artifact new to the adopting or recipient unit. The first stage in the Zaltman model is initiation, consisting of knowledge awareness and decision, which is followed by a stage of implementation. Innovation is regarded as an organizational process, but it is treated as a static variable that is either adopted or rejected. Components of the environment are considered in the selection of an innovation but not in how it is reshaped during the implementation stage.

My own research (DiBella, 1992) suggests that there is another outcome for practice diffusion, one involving reinterpretation and adaptation. Decision and choice are not attributes of the initiation stage alone but of implementation as well. The factors that shape those choices lie at several levels and are both internal and external to the organization.

Managers may try to improve performance by learning "best practices" that are perceived to have been effective elsewhere. This scenario is precisely what occurs when teams or their parent institutions learn (or try to learn) from one another. As an effort at planned change, such initiatives progress through a series of stages (described in the following section) that, combined, produce adaptation (see Fig. 7-2).

Figure 7-2
Stage Model of "Best Practice" Learning and Adaptation

Importation ➤ Definition ➤ Modification ➤ Identification ➤ Absorption

Stages of "Best Practice" Learning and Adaptation

Importation

First, an individual or team decides to improve performance or solve some problem by identifying and learning a practice or technique that is perceived to work elsewhere. Such practices may come to the attention of the recipient from a group that is part of the same organization or firm (internal Knowledge Source) or from one that lies beyond it (external Knowledge Source). Through some mode of transfer or communication, details of the practice become known to the recipient team.

Many firms that see the value in organizational learning and want to leverage the experience and mistakes of one group for another are now creating on-line computer-based repositories of lessons learned. Consulting firms, especially those that regard intellectual property and knowledge management as core capabilities, are trying to learn from their own project activities; they make the lessons they have learned available to others. A critical presumption is that if repositories of lessons learned by certain teams are created (public Knowledge Reserve), they will subsequently be imported by others. However, it is one thing to store and disseminate information about some practice, it is quite another to learn or replicate that practice or lesson in another setting.

Definition

This stage involves the development of an insider's (recipient) interpretation of exactly what the practice is, how it works, and what its expected outcomes are. Such an interpretation or reinterpretation derives in part from how the practice to be learned relates to what the recipients already know or do. This stage may involve relabeling or renaming the practice to enhance recognition. Since the imported practice emerged from the culture or experience of another team or social group, the importing (recipient) team must develop its own shared meaning about the practice. Without a shared meaning and interpretation in the team, there is no common ground for collective action. (For example, what may seem an obvious learned lesson in one group may be perceived as a threat to the stability of another.)

A first step in the definition stage is for team members to discuss how implementing the practice can lead to certain benefits and how the practice is supposed to work in theory, as evidenced in its use by the originator. Such conversations can sensitize recipients to the key assumptions underlying the practice and can help them determine whether such assumptions are valid in their own team or corporate culture. For example, underlying any work practice are assumptions about how or why team members are motivated, how specific behaviors or tasks produce valued outcomes (and how long it takes to do so), and what are the expected consequences. Recipients need to reflect on how cultural differences between their team and the originating team can make following the practice, as it was initially designed, have unintended and undesirable consequences.

Modification

During this stage, design changes are made in various components or aspects of the practice to enhance its perceived value within the recipient team or organization. For example, user qualifications can be modified to take team members' backgrounds into consideration; frequency of use can be adjusted to the needs of the team and the expected benefits; and rewards for following the practice can be adjusted to what team members value and are willing to work for. As changes are made to the practice, recipients make their mark on it and begin to value the practice as their own.

Identification

With adjustments made and the practice tried out, staff come to accept the innovation and to further develop their own shared meanings of its value. Additional changes and modifications are made as the practice is diffused to other teams or company settings. Use occurs because the recipients are able to redefine or reconfigure the practice into something that holds meaning for them, and this meaning is further reinforced through use.

Absorption

Over time and through additional changes the re-innovation or emulated practice becomes part of a standard repertoire of practices. As such it becomes routinized and domesticated, and no longer subject to critical review. What was learned becomes taken for granted and transparent to the users. As such, learned practices become part of the team or company culture and are regarded as "how we do things around here."

Keys to Successful Adaptation

By the time a practice has progressed through these five stages, it is no longer an innovation or someone else's "best practice." Over time the practice, its design, and perhaps its purpose as well are transformed into something different. It is no longer something to be learned (except by new members of the recipient system) or replicated but an accepted way of doing things, and may itself become a focus for subsequent innovation. The key is that the practice, however it has been reshaped or transformed through adaptation, becomes part of the team's or organization's repertoire of behaviors or processes. (Levitt & March [1988] characterize this process as "encoding history into routines that guide behavior.")

The greater the cultural disparity between the originating and recipient team, the greater the need for adaptation. Without that, the practice may be rejected with incumbents returning to their traditional forms of behavior as in the example from the Peace Corps. If the modifications made to the practice have been modest relative to the cultural disparity between the originating and recipient systems, the practice may create conflict rather than address the problem that first led the team to use a "best practice."

Learning across team and other corporate boundaries is expedited through the adaptation process, and understanding this process of adaptation and practice diffusion is itself an opportunity for organizational learning. In Chapters 5 and 6 a variety of suggestions were offered about ways to build learning capability. These practices are not very detailed since experience has shown that the more detailed the prescription or suggestion, the lower the chance of its being adapted, and hence adopted. The more specific or ironclad the practice is, the less opportunity there is for recipient users to place their own mark on the practice. Practices that seem incomplete or are underspecified bring the user in, from a gestalt point of view, to complete the picture and thereby build in details of the practice.

The inventories of learning practices presented in Chapters 5 and 6 represent suggested, possible ways to promote learning or shift learning approaches. To apply these suggestions successfully depends on the adaptive capability of teams and organizations that seek to emulate or use "best practices." The notion of "best practice" is unfortunately a constraining one since it presumes that there is one best way. That view may deter adaptation, make learning a singular rather than a pluralistic set of practices, and reduce the number of perceived learning choices. One key in adapting learning practices is not to reduce their number to only the ones somehow or someway regarded as "best," but to improve recipients' judgment so that they are able to select from a wider range of choices. Viewing these choices from a portfolio framework is the focus of the next chapter.

Learning Practices: Lesson 7

Cultural differences between teams and workgroups will be reflected in what and how they learn. When borrowing practices, allow the adaptation process to occur to build team identification and ownership.

Part III

The Advantaged Learner

There are many learning advocates in the world, but the world also has its share of skeptics. Learning requires organizational resources (time, money, energy) that can be used for other purposes, and learning can lead to change that is disquieting if not downright troublesome. Thus it's not enough to identify a team's or organization's learning profile as we did in Part I or to consider practices that alter or enhance profiles as we did in Part II. The advantaged learner allocates resources in such a way as to maximize their benefit while successfully confronting several critical challenges.

In this final section we will examine how workers, managers, and their organizations can maximize the benefits of learning. Chapter 8 looks at a company as a learning portfolio and at how companies can improve their allocation of learning investments. Chapter 9 examines a set of critical challenges that practitioners face as they try to learn "best practices." Chapter 10 discusses how time and space affect our perceptions of learning and how new information and communication technologies are altering the nature of those constraints.

8

Making Learning Investments: Learning Portfolios and Architectures

Time discovers truth.
—Seneca

In this chapter we will consider the notion of a company or organization as a learning portfolio and the implications for managing that portfolio to its maximum advantage. If we build up from the idea that different groups or subsystems within an organization or firm have different learning profiles, then the entire system has an aggregate set of these profiles. This set of profiles (and the learning styles represented therein) constitutes its learning portfolio. When organizations invest in learning, they choose, whether explicitly or not, to emphasize certain elements, practices, or styles in their portfolios.

This chapter examines the criteria that should guide firms in making learning investments. In that process, I introduce two additional characteristics or dimensions (Learning Impact and Learning Use) that can guide learning investments. Companies that understand their own knowledge needs can design learning architectures that embed learning processes as part of an organization's structure or culture.

Foundations of Learning Portfolios

As should be clear from the extended lists of learning practices included in Chapters 5 and 6, there are many ways that teams and organizations learn. Teams learn both in collective ways, as when explicit knowledge is shared among team members or across organizational units, and in personal ways, as when the tacit knowledge of individual team members increases. In aggregate, the pattern of these practices shapes learning styles and orientations. An organization's capability to learn in different ways is like an individual's ability to speak many languages. To characterize the nature of this capability, we could allude to the pluralism of organizational learning. Individuals are far more adaptable when they are multilingual; in the same way, organizations that support various learning activities can learn in different contexts and can better adapt what is learned in other contexts.

This condition of learning pluralism is further reflected in the existence of different learning profiles across different teams, work units, or subsystems of some larger organization or firm.The total sum of learning approaches and practices in these profiles represents the organization's learning portfolio. The more ways a team or company learns, the broader its learning portfolio, and the greater the chance that learning will occur serendipitously or synergistically. This progression or aggregation of learning is depicted in Figure 8-1.

When we recognize a firm's learning portfolio, we take a whole-systems view of the firm's capability. Such a perspective enables management to examine the fit between specific approaches and profiles and between the entire portfolio and the surrounding environment of the firm. With this bird's-eye view, management is in a position to examine the distribution of resources within the portfolio.

Analyzing Learning Portfolios

When we look at a firm's learning portfolio in its entirety, several questions and concerns come to mind. First, what's in the portfolio now? Answering this question requires having an inventory of the learning practices and profiles that exist throughout the organization or firm. This inventory of data about learning provides the basic building blocks for analysis.

A second concern pertains to the relatedness of the items in the inventory. To what extent are the learning approaches, orientations, and profiles complementary, in conflict, or redundant? For example, in Chapter 4, I discussed the complementarity in nuclear power plants of having a research and development unit engaged in transformative learning practices while incremental learning takes place among operations staff.

Figure 8-1

Components of a Learning Portfolio

On the other hand, when two teams that learn through their own experiences (internal Knowledge Source) in informal ways (informal Dissemination Mode) are asked to formally collaborate with one another, conflicts are bound to develop. Neither team would be likely to value the knowledge of the other. Learning redundancies occur in organizations when teams use limited resources to duplicate similar learning, or as the saying goes, to reinvent the wheel.

A third concern about learning portfolios is the extent to which current practices or styles align with or match learning needs and work demands. Consider a team or organization that is in a new industry where innovation is critical to success. If it has an overemphasis on learning practices that support formal Dissemination Mode or incremental Learning Scope, then what's getting learned (and the speed whereby that learning is disseminated) is not apt to be as helpful to the firm's competitiveness as practices that support transformative learning. In another scenario, if a firm wants to emphasize teamwork, then it should give more support to learning practices that promote group rather than individual Learning Focus.

The idea that a firm's learning portfolio might be misaligned with its learning needs or competitive demands raises questions about portfolio management. How can a firm manage its portfolio for maximum advantage? What criteria should be followed in making portfolio management decisions? How would a managed learning portfolio differ from an unmanaged one? These questions suggest that instead of blindly supporting learning practices or not supporting them at all, companies might allocate their learning resources within their portfolio in such a way so as to maximize their effectiveness. Learning capability and learning effectiveness must go hand in hand.

Learning Portfolio Management

Managing a learning portfolio requires a sensitivity and an appreciation for outcomes. Traditionally, in most business environments, outcomes or outputs are examined in light of inputs. Return on investment, or ROI, has been a key measure or statistic that reflects the ratio of outputs to inputs. The greater the output relative to the same input, the higher the ROI. Since businesspeople aim to maximize the returns on their investments, they make management decisions about their investments using ROI as a guiding criterion.

Using ROI as a singular criterion for making management or investment decisions, however, is a limiting approach. To determine the value of outputs and expected returns requires that assumptions be made about the future, and these assumptions can turn out to be invalid. Assumptions are also made about linear associations, that an investment (usually financial resources) will be converted to some measurable amount of inputs (material, labor, process technology) that will in turn be converted to an expected set of outputs (products, services, benefits). Over time unanticipated events or circumstances occur that thwart the realization of the presumed causal linkage, as when the cost of material or labor increases. Consequently, many management decisions end up being based on projections that turn out to be inaccurate.

This problem is especially prevalent with learning investments since the period during which the returns from learning are realized can be quite lengthy, and the lengthier the period of returns to be gained from an investment, the more uncertain we must be about our assumptions. Also the usefulness of learning pertains to its timeliness. When we learn something in a formal training program, such as how to use new software for group collaboration, it's often because we expect to use these new skills right away. In that scenario, the benefits and outcomes from the learning have immediate value. On the other hand, we sometimes learn behaviors (such as how to deal with angry customers or aggressive competitors) that we hope we never have to use. If we never use such behaviors, does that mean they have no value and were not worth the initial learning investment? Of course not, but what criteria should we use to make decisions among such learning investments?

Another difficulty in using ROI as a criterion to manage learning investments is that it only takes into account tangible assets or returns. When an employee learns a new skill, a workteam learns how to work better together or a firm develops a new process technology, nothing tangible is created, but the learning has obviously produced something of value. When managers take the established route of basing investment decisions and allocating learning resources among practices that promise a higher ROI, they miss several critical characteristics of learning.

Investment Dimensions to Learning

There are two critical aspects or dimensions to learning that have direct bearing on learning portfolio management. The first of these, which I have named "Learning Use," came to my attention while researching and working with clients in the health care field. The second, Learning Impact, came from my consulting work in the education industry.

1. *Learning Use*

Some of the learning that takes place in health care involves practices or techniques that are used immediately to care for sick patients. Health care is a unique context in which the effect of not learning (possible death of the patient) can be devastating. Consequently, medical practitioners and caregivers continually explore new procedures and protocols. They learn new techniques because they are needed immediately, and as part of their formal training they learn established techniques to treat illnesses and diseases they may encounter at some future date.

One can think of this difference in learning approaches as reflecting a time dimension to the value of learning. With some practices, the usefulness of what's been learned is realized in the short term, while with others, the benefit comes later. In industry this contrast is reflected in a manager's choice between focusing on production activities that create valued outcomes and benefits in the short term and investment activities that lead to benefits in the long term. This contrast is depicted in the following continuum:

Learning Use: immediate . . . . future

The relative timeliness of when we use or apply what we have learned is an important criterion to weigh in choosing between alternative learning investments. Whether this characteristic or criterion represents another robust Learning Orientation beyond the seven identified from my previous research remains to be determined. In the meantime considering a practice in light of its learning use (immediate vs. future) is a helpful marker.

2. *Learning Impact*

It is one thing to use or apply what we have learned, it is another to realize the benefits from that use. For example, while a health care practitioner may learn and then use a new protocol to assist someone who is in poor health, whether the use of that protocol actually adds value or creates benefit to the patient may not be known for some time. In effect, there are time lags between the use of learning and its resultant benefits. Consequently, we can't be certain, at the outset, of the value of what we're learning.

For some uses of learning, the benefits are unambiguous, as when emergency-room staff use new protocols to save a patient. In other cases, such as cancer treatment, whether a new form of surgery or a new protocol of radiation therapy will extend the life of a patient may not be known until some time has passed. We must also be uncertain of the impact when learned attitudes or behaviors are used without controls or comparisons. Without the latter we cannot be sure that the outcomes should be attributed to what had just been learned or to some other factor, such as chance or the passage of time. For example, if a sick patient is treated with some technique recently learned by medical staff and then feels better, we cannot be sure that the patient would not have felt better anyway without the new treatment.

Thus while learning may be used immediately, the payoff from that use may be uncertain or lag behind in time. Often we learn and use new behaviors because their impact is empirically known. At other times the impact is unknown, but we invest in learning just the same because we believe that the payoff or benefit will ultimately be positive. This contrast is depicted in the following continuum:

Learning Impact: certain . . . . uncertain

The field of education is forever having to cope with the challenges of this dichotomy. In our large research universities, scholars who teach focus on developing theory whose impact is uncertain, while many of their students prefer learning that they perceive will have a proven impact. In primary and secondary education we invest in the schooling of our children with the hope and expectation that they will learn how to have meaningful lives as adults. Of course, support for education also comes from competitive pressures for our children to be as successful as possible (even as other competitive pressures lead investors to expect our corporations to be as profitable as possible). The uncertain but expected payoffs from elementary and secondary education help fuel the coffers of many local school committees.

Yet when it comes to supporting education or learning in corporate environments, decision makers aren't quite so generous since they rely on ROI and other business measures to assess the returns and value of investments in learning. Learning portfolio management aims to maximize that value. Considering the Learning Use and Learning Impact of a given practice can guide that process and ensure the effectiveness of learning efforts.

Assessing Learning Effectiveness

To be learning effectively means investing and allocating resources to learning practices that maximize value. Assessing learning effectiveness involves identifying the impact of practices in one's learning portfolio. We can refer to Learning Use and Learning Impact as markers in assessing impact. Any learning practice can be scored on the basis of these two dimensions to determine *relative* value. (*Relative* is highlighted for emphasis since absolute value cannot be determined;

our focus should be on weighing the value of learning investments compared to one another.) Once practices are scored, learning resources can be allocated on the basis of those scores.

For companies or organizations to benefit from this approach, a first step would be to rate the LU and LI of all the practices in their learning portfolios. Both LU and LI can be rated on a 10-point scale. For example, the greater the known impact of the practice, the higher the rating, and the more immediate the use of the practice, the higher the rating. Consequently, "immediate" Learning Use rates a "10," as does "certain" Learning Impact. "Future" use and "uncertain" impact would each rate a "1."

Once the LU and LI of a practice are rated, the score of the practice can be determined by multiplying those two ratings. The maximum score is 100, the minimum 1. Chart 8-1 provides a format to show the scores of a company's or organization's learning practices. Practices may be rank ordered in terms of their score from highest to lowest. Decisions about allocating learning resources can be based on that ranking, among other criteria.

Another way to view the scoring data is to plot them on a graph. Figure 8-2 presents a graph that juxtaposes Learning Use and Learning Impact, with LU represented on the horizontal axis and LI on the vertical axis. By transposing the scores from Chart 8-1 onto this graph, we can see how a company's or organization's learning practices cluster and can use the results to guide decisions about resource allocation. In general, any practice that is mapped onto the upper-left quadrant should have high priority for investment; practices that map onto the lower-left or the upper-right quadrant would have medium priority; and practices that map onto the lower-right quadrant would have low priority.

There are other ways to use or view these data for making learning investment decisions. Rather than simply looking at how distinct learning practices map onto the graph, we can take a gestalt or systems view of the entire portfolio and look for aggregate patterns or clusters. For example, should most or all of a firm's learning practices fit into one quadrant or toward one end of either axis, we could consider whether that clustering best suits the work demands and competitive pressures on the company.

Ideally, any pattern should reflect both the company's strategic emphasis and the relative priority it places among alternative learning practices or investments. (This priority will vary from one firm to another since LU and LI would be just two among a set of other data

Chart 8-1
Learning Practice Scoring Table

Learning Practice (a...............z)	Learning Use (1–10)	Learning Impact (1–10)	Score (LU × LI: 1–100)

Key:

Learning Use (LU):   10.........5.........1
                      immediate ....future

Learning Impact (LI):   10.........5.........1
                         certain.....................uncertain

points or criteria used to allocate learning resources.) Consider, for example, a company where the majority of its learning practices focused on immediate use and certain outcomes (upper-left quadrant). If the firm decided to shift its corporate strategy so that it might better compete for the future through innovation (Hamel & Prahalad, 1994), then its learning resources should be reallocated to the right side of the graph to reflect that shift. Other firms that might view strategy

Figure 8-2
Graph of Learning Practice Scores

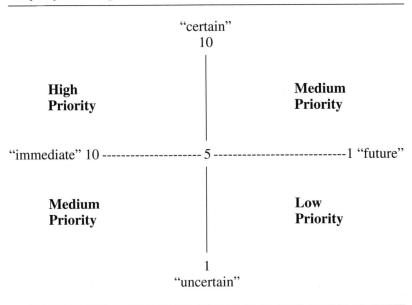

development and implementation as structured uncertainty or chaos (Brown & Eisenhardt, 1998) would shift their investments toward practices that would map onto the lower end of the graph.

Learning Use and Learning Impact and their juxtaposition can be used to guide a firm in understanding its learning effectiveness and in managing its learning portfolio. Learning priorities will vary between firms due to competitive pressures and cultural differences. Yet they ultimately establish a firm's learning architecture, which becomes the transparent structure that shapes what a company and its employees learn.

Supporting Learning Architectures: The Role of Chief Learning Officer

After a company allocates its learning investments, patterns of learning activity are created that culminate in the establishment of the company's learning portfolio. In building up from practices and orientations to profiles and portfolios, as we have in previous chapters, we assessed and analyzed already existing learning activities. We also considered how portfolios might be altered to better align learning with the strategic needs of the firm.

As we shape a firm's learning portfolio, we effectively work as learning architects with the hope that what we design will ultimately be realized. Many firms have come to recognize the need to take a systems view of learning and to proactively shape their learning architecture. For this reason, many firms have created corporate universities to oversee all learning activities. Other firms have developed roles for learning strategists and chief learning officers (CLOs).

(Companies that are oriented toward the use of computers or information technology to promote learning have created the role of chief knowledge officer (CKO). In some cases the transition to this role involved merely relabeling previous job titles, such as chief information officer or director of management information systems. In general, the focus of these latter positions is on managing and utilizing existing computerized databases through data mining rather than on learning portfolio management.)

The role of the CLO is more comprehensive to, in effect, oversee a company's learning architecture and ensure that what's in the portfolio actually matches the architecture. To do so involves several activities intended to design, develop, and maintain learning. The first is the task of designing the learning architecture in light of the organization's culture and learning demands. A CLO should take a comprehensive view of an organization or firm to understand its learning requirements and to profile current and desired learning. (Taking such a perspective is consistent with steps 1 and 2 of an OD approach as presented in Chapter 1.) The second task is supporting those learning practices that are required to meet the firm's strategic needs. The third task is to evaluate practices for their quality and impact and to redesign the learning architecture as necessary.

Many firms have given their CLOs the role of running their corporate universities. Unfortunately, the activities of corporate universities emphasize practices that engender formal learning such as training and classroom teaching. The domain of a strategically focused CLO is on all learning practices and on how to allocate learning resources among them.

With a systems view, a CLO looks comprehensively at a firm's learning portfolio, sees how it aligns with the strategic demands on the firm, and allocates resources accordingly. Yet perhaps more importantly, the role of the CLO is to be an organization's or firm's learning advocate. As we transition more and more into the postindustrial age and into a services economy, companies are placing greater emphasis on knowledge management. When firms learn by creating or acquiring knowledge, they develop a growing capacity for effective action. It is difficult to place a value on that capacity since it is an intangible asset; a CLO must champion the allocation and use of resources that produce such intangible assets.

Learning Use and Learning Impact are important markers in allocating resources among alternative learning practices. Yet it is the value created from learning practices that many managers view as the ultimate criterion. A challenge facing many CLOs is to promote learning, which in many cases creates intangible assets, in contexts that place value only on what is tangible. However, a CLO faces many other critical challenges in realizing a firm's architecture and to these we turn in the next chapter.

Learning Practices: Lesson 8

An organization's learning portfolio represents its collection of learning practices. A critical role for chief learning officers is to assure that resources allocated within the portfolio maximize learning effectiveness and promote strategic results.

9

Critical Challenges in Learning "Best Practices"

Never let formal education get in the way of your learning.
—Mark Twain

Throughout this book, I've presented ideas and analytical tools to develop learning capability in teams and organizations. There are, however, several critical challenges that practitioners face as they focus on, develop, and use so-called "best practices." In this chapter I suggest ways to reexamine or rethink the nature of these challenges.

The Spotlight on "Best Practices"

This week, like most weeks, I received several marketing brochures about upcoming professional conferences. One brochure, for a conference about starting a corporate university, was subtitled "Best Practices in Management, Measurement, and Marketing." Another was for a conference on running training departments as if they were businesses and was subtitled "Best Practices, Straight Talk." It seems as if everywhere I go, I hear the expression "best practices." But what are "best practices," and why is the business world so occupied in searching for them?

The business world is a context rich in dichotomies: profit/loss, labor/management, success/failure, products/services, headquarters/field, control/chaos, culture/structure. It's as if the world was either black or white, good or bad. From this and a host of other cultural values springs the notion that there is some apex or optimal condition that must be emulated to ensure corporate success: If companies just did what's best, their problems would be solved, if not completely eliminated. This tendency is epitomized in the desire to find the magic bullet, create the right corporate culture, or make the quick fix. The idea seems to exist that if companies could just locate and somehow store these fixes or "best practices," then they will have established a permanent foundation for excellence and profitability. Several prominent management consulting firms have responded to this by highlighting their efforts to inventory "global best practices," as if management "best practices" were solutions as generic as hand tools and other material devices that can be used effectively by anyone, anywhere. Such presumed universality can be deceptive since it implies either avoidance or undervaluation of unique local conditions, and because, quite simply, life is not all black and white. For this reason wherever I have referred to so-called "best practices," I have placed the words in quotes.

All management practices are based on a set of assumptions about desirable outcomes and the specific processes or behaviors that need to be followed in order to reach those outcomes. However, a practice that is labeled best because it is valued and works well in a particular setting may meet different constraints, limitations, and circumstances in other settings. (As the saying from Descartes goes, "truths on one side of the Pyrenees are falsehoods on the other.") For example, while some corporations may strive to maximize profits, others may seek to maximize customer satisfaction, product quality, or benefits to some wider community. Goals are usually not singular but multiple and are often in conflict. Criteria to assess goal achievement may likewise vary. A practice that is valued in one setting will be valued differently in another setting where different goals have priority. A practice that works well in a corporate setting where the focus is on quarterly profits, for example, is not apt to work best in a nonprofit setting that aims to maximize overall social benefits.

The valuation of practices across different settings is also affected by how organizations relate to time. Some organizations (and entire industries) are short-term focused, while others have a long-term orientation. There are also time lags between the use of practices and their outcomes, and these lags will vary between organizations. What may make a practice best in the short term can, from a systems dynamic perspective, make it dysfunctional in the long term. For example, a management practice that produces short-term profitability can lead to long-term employee morale problems. Likewise, downsizing initiatives may reduce short-term headcount and labor costs but be detrimental to future growth and employee loyalty in the long run.

Another aspect of the time dimension to "best practices" is that as innovation occurs, practices become dated. Changes in economics, individual preferences, technology, or ways of thinking provide a different foundation from which entirely new practices can emerge. Such innovations aren't improvements of old, now out-of-date, once "best practices" but are based on entirely new paradigms. Anyone overly attached to the old practice may be slow, or unable, to transition to the new one.

Thus to think in terms of "best practice" can be misleading if not counter-productive, and to place an overemphasis on archiving "best practices" may be a foolish pursuit. That is not to say that we can't learn from the past or from others. However, it is oversimplifying to think that we can identify, archive, and then retrieve universal "best practices" whenever we want.

The challenge lies in balancing generic possibilities with local realities. Managers and practitioners need to recognize and respect local idiosyncrasies without becoming myopic. Otherwise, we risk discrediting or overlooking conditions that are essential to success and alienating ourselves from those we wish to support. If we are too enmeshed in local realities, we may not be open to other ideas or ways of working. Balancing involves searching for solutions without becoming mesmerized by the success of others. Another part of this balancing act is being committed to and focused on practices that work well now while still being open to new practices that may work better tomorrow. New practices aren't necessarily better because they seem innovative or have become popular.

An overreliance on searching for "best practices" in management, marketing, training, learning, or whatever the area of concern can lead to a psychological dependence in finding solutions outside of ourselves or our own organizations. A more productive orientation is to balance an appreciation for the old with an openness for the new. We must also recognize that there are no absolute or universal "best practices" but there are generic possibilities that require adaptation to local conditions.

Moving from "Best Practices" to "Best Principles"

The absence of absolute "best practices" suggests that a focus on "best learning practices" may be too specific or narrow. Instead of looking for or developing and then learning "best practices," it would seem more productive to consider the nature of "best principles." Several authors have already taken this approach in trying to identify what makes for great companies or productive working relationships among them. In their groundbreaking book about excellence, Peters and Waterman (1982) identified eight "attributes" of successful companies. Some of them, such as "close to the customer" and "stick to the knitting," have become rallying cries for some companies. More recently, Collins and Porras (1994) discussed their research on the *fundamental principles* of visionary companies, including "homegrown management" and "preserve the core." Yet the search for key principles has not been focused on the firm level alone. In continuing his elaboration of what makes for successful process consultation, Schein (1999a) identified five principles, including "access your ignorance" and "the client owns the problem and solution." These authors emphasize general direction over technique: while they discuss practices consistent with their principles, they omit specifying how these principles are realized. That task requires the kind of reflection and involvement among practitioners that fosters adaptation, identification, and a sense of ownership.

In Part II of this book, I described a variety of practices that promote or represent learning. Yet throughout this book, I have discussed a general approach to learning that can be articulated in a set of learning principles. While I am reluctant to promote "best learning practices," I do advocate the following as "best learning principles."

Principle 1. Treat Learning As a Change or OD Intervention

Learning is a revolutionary process that challenges the status quo. Teams and organizations with established cultures can easily be threatened by new knowledge or new behaviors. Learning requires a letting go or change from the past, a process that some (Nystrom & Starbuck, 1984) refer to as "unlearning." However you label it, learning involves change, whether in or of some system, and is thus best treated as a type of intervention. Building strategic learning capability in teams and organizations requires adherence to some framework for promoting change; the OD book series in which this volume appears offers many model frameworks to choose from.

Principle 2. Honor the Many Forms and Styles of Learning

Just as culture comes in many forms, so too does learning. Different forms of learning should be looked upon as sources of potential synergy rather than of potential conflict. Understanding and tolerance of differences can produce innovation and rich learning architectures.

Principle 3. Modify Learning Through Adaptation

No idea or practice is as good as one's own; ownership comes from taking an idea or practice and reshaping it to one's own preferences, idiosyncrasies, and conditions. When we learn from others, we develop ownership through the process of adaptation. What we learn also has to be adapted over time as the context and conditions of use change.

Principle 4. Distinguish Learning Content from Learning Processes

While it is important to advocate for learning, we need to distinguish between what we learn and our learning process and ability to learn. If we learn what is contrary to our needs or goals, we are not being either productive or strategic in our use of what are in most cases limited resources for learning. We can develop learning capability, but we must also be mindful of how that capability is being applied and directed.

These four principles have provided me with a sense of direction in working with clients to develop learning capability. While we might argue over whose practices (yours, mine, our competitors, etc.) are better, it is more difficult to do so with principles. The challenge is to be aware of one's often unarticulated principles and to use them for selecting learning actions and practices. As a point of reflection, can you state your learning principles?

Learning in the Context of Change

Focusing on and being aware of one's principles is important since practices are apt to change over time, while principles are more robust. How we learn and what we learn must shift as the context for learning changes. A changing environment has become a fundamental characteristic of our society and our organizations. This dynamic of learning in the context of change provides another challenge.

Given the speed and regularity of change in society, we are frequently faced with the task of learning something that may very soon be eclipsed by something else. Where do we find the motivation and resources to learn something today that might be out-of-date tomorrow? How do we confront the challenge of learning and developing an identification with knowledge or behaviors whose value may be ephemeral?

Here we apply Principle 1 to acknowledge that learning and change are interwoven, continuous processes. Learning means confronting the certainty and apparent structure of today with the ambiguity and chaos of tomorrow, and resolving that tension through ongoing change. This balancing of what we know with what we need to know, of structure with chaos (a condition that Dee Hock (1999) has termed "chaordic") requires clarity of purpose and confidence of spirit.

One skill that helps in meeting this challenge is improvisation. This skill requires the ability to let go of the past in order to meet the requirements of the present. The improvisationalist must react in novel ways to whatever circumstances arise to in effect learn-in-action. A wonderful example of learning and change through improvisation is the experience of the flight crew aboard Apollo 13. You may recall that in 1973 Apollo 13 was scheduled to land on the moon. An explosion aboard the spacecraft required the crew to throw out their flight plan and develop a range of elaborate and unanticipated procedures to return safely to Earth.

Learning and improvisation are like muscles that will atrophy if not used. The more we exercise our ability to learn, the more confident we become to cope with chaos and change and to improvise. When we are confronted with uncertainty, we have little, if any, time for reflection or analysis. However, if we have confidence, we can trust in our instinct to learn-in-action and to succeed.

Finding Time for Reflection

While chaotic conditions give us no time for reflection, another challenge is finding time for reflection and activities that promote learning even when conditions are stable. The frenzied pace of life in many organizations and the emphasis on today's production leave little time for such seemingly unproductive activities as learning. The challenge is how to put learning on our schedules.

This challenge is exacerbated by a cultural predisposition in industrialized societies, especially in the United States, toward action. The tendency, as the saying goes, is "Don't just stand there, do something." Managers who take time to reflect on a situation may be subject to claims that they are indecisive or suffer "paralysis from analysis." (Conversely, where time is seemingly abundant, the glut of available information in computerized management information systems may overwhelm our ability to process and make sense of it.)

One way of coping with multiple demands amidst limited time and resources is multitasking. For example, I often read the newspaper when eating breakfast and listen to audiotapes while driving to client engagements. Managers don't just have a meal in the middle of the day, they have lunch meetings. Other people eat meals while driving their cars, watch cable news television while exercising on treadmills, and use cell-phones while doing just about anything.

One way that scholars have made the connection between learning and multitasking is by developing innovative techniques such as thinking-in-action (Schon, 1984), action science (Argyris, 1985), and work-based learning (Raelin, 1999). We learn from and through our own actions by concurrently engaging our reflective, analytical, and doing selves. Such approaches can be far less demanding on organizations than on individuals. One part of an organization may be engaged in operational activity while another part is engaged in learning and reflection. For this reason expansive corporate learning architectures and portfolios are important. Our challenge is to focus and learn amidst the apparent chaos of changing circumstances and to make time for learning amidst the demands of our everyday obligations. The final chapter looks at ways that companies are meeting these challenges.

Learning Practices: Lesson 9

Developing "best principles" is apt to be a more productive pursuit than searching for "best practices." Given the constraint of time and the demands placed on us by a changing world, we need to learn through both reflection and improvisation.

10

The Learning Horizon

Learning is like rowing upstream;
not to advance is to drop back.

—Chinese proverb

Linking Learning, Time, and Space

Time and space are fundamental dimensions of any endeavor. Learning and time are associated in several unique ways, as when we take time now to learn something specific, like CPR (cardiopulmonary resuscitation), that we may need to use in an emergency tomorrow. We also invest in learning to develop something new for the future, such as an innovative product or service. If what management thinkers (deGeus, 1988) and practitioners (Stata, 1989) say is true, that learning has become the critical capability that organizations will need over time to survive, then we have to be mindful of the time dimension of learning.

Traditional forms of learning, such as classroom teaching, have historically been constrained by the parameters of space, such as the number of students that can fit into a lecture hall or seminar room. Similarly, learning within a workteam that is not colocated has been limited by the physical separation, distance, or space between its members. However, technical achievements in our era are redefining how we think about or use space as a dimension of any learning experience. As we envision our learning horizon, this chapter looks at new possibilities in the links between learning, time, and space.

The Evolving Nature of Learning

Consistent with Principle 4 as presented in Chapter 9, space and time differentially affect what we learn and how we learn. Some of these differences relate to cultural distinctions as described in the anthropological examinations of time and space by Edward Hall (1959, 1966). Learning methods evolve over time as technology and patterns of thinking and interaction change; what we learn or need to learn evolves as we accumulate experience and as the world places different demands on us and our organizations.

For example, over time we develop a more refined understanding of the physical world around us and the inner world of our own experience. Through continual redefinition, evolution, and adaptation of meaning, we shift learning priorities in terms of what we need to learn. On an individual level, we can think about how evolving notions about intelligence have affected employee and management development. The recognition of the importance of multiple intelligence and emotional intelligence as contributors to job performance has led to different learning content and priorities in employee-training programs. On an institutional level, the development of the Internet as a vehicle for communication with customers and clients has required sales personnel to learn different forms of marketing.

As the nature of our existence and of organizational life changes, so too do the demands placed on our learning capability. Our learning must not only keep up with these demands but must anticipate them as well. That means we must keep an eye on our learning horizon and build organizational learning capability that is in tune with how organizations and their employees create meaning and economic value.

Learning about general trends, such as changes in societal demographics or global climate, provides insight into the demands of tomorrow. That insight can help us to shift priorities for learning content in advance of what's to come. (For example, changing demographics have implications for organizations in terms of staff recruitment, retention, and retirement. If a company learns that the age distribution of its employee-candidate pool is changing, it can alter its hiring practices to reduce the impact of that change.) Yet the value of whatever we learn is inexorably linked to time; intellectual gains make anachronisms out of what was previously learned.

The Learning Time Line

As we gain experience over time that adds to our knowledge or as we acquire knowledge about future trends, we develop the capability to enhance our performance in the present and future. However, in most organizational systems there are time lags that affect the application of learning. Having knowledge usually predates the ability to put that knowledge into action. Thus time relates to learning through both the sources and uses of our knowledge.

One way to consider the relationship between time and learning is through the use of a learning time line, such as the following:

Learning Time Line

| past | present | future |

The learning time line suggests the time range in both the source and use of our learning. An organization's learning portfolio should represent learning investments that are distributed throughout the time line. Some parts of an organization may conduct debriefing of events and experiences in order to learn from the past, while other parts may examine trends to draw a picture of the future and its learning horizon. Operations staff improvise or apply learning in the present, while new product developers apply learning whose value is not realized until their new product comes to market sometime in the future.

With regard to the time dimension of our sources of learning, learning about and from the past means learning from experience, whether our own or someone else's. Yet the meaning and value of past experiences shifts as we progress through the time line. Past events come to be understood in different ways because of what we now know in the present or about the future. Consequently, the process of debriefing past events, or learning opportunities, as described in Chapter 5, can be revisited multiple times to produce additional insight and learning.

The ability to learn in the present represents just-in-time learning (JITL); improvisation is the ability to use what we are learning to adapt to circumstances as they occur. JITL is a very expedient, yet difficult process. It's difficult because it occurs when we have no time for reflection or when we face a situation that demands immediate action. It's expedient because we learn in and through our actions, a form of multitasking, to maximize value gained.

With regard to learning in and for the future, although we can't live in the future, we can project being there or anticipate it based on present trends. (Science fiction, the genre of writing that propels the reader into possible future scenarios, may also serve as a source of insight and learning.) The challenge is learning how to better predict or anticipate the future, recognize previously unanticipated challenges, and find new ways to see into the future. Learning about and for the future has, like other positions along the time line, implications for both content and process that need to be recognized and developed.

A major time constraint in the ability of organizations to learn has been the fixed length of their workday. Productivity typically declines over the course of the workday due to employee fatigue. Global corporations have been able to circumvent this constraint by putting together workteams that operate in different time zones and whose workdays run sequentially rather than concurrently. The activities of such teams go on independent of the time limitations of any one team or team member.

It is not by chance that the world's major consulting and accounting firms have offices and employees spread throughout Planet Earth. This structural characteristic allows firms to better service local clients (by reducing the time needed to meet or communicate with them) and to continue project work unabated and unconstrained by the length of the workday at any one work site. Shared computer programs and files provide team members in one time zone with access to the work of team members in other time zones.

Learning Space

Learning and other tasks performed by geographically dispersed workteams demonstrate how time and space are intertwined. With geographically dispersed workteams, firms can debrief and analyze learning events and opportunities on a round-the-clock basis, but that is not the only way that the constraints of time and space have been altered. New computer technologies and computer programs have completely opened up new domains to promote learning in organizational settings. In this final section, we will look briefly at how the dimension of space relates to learning and then discover what's possible today to circumvent or reinvent spacial limitations.

As described earlier, we can reflect on the notion of space and how traditional forms of learning (and schooling) take place in such diverse settings as classrooms, lecture halls, seminar rooms, and laboratories, or during nature walks in the woods. Such spaces provide forums or venues to generate or share knowledge. They are also important in demarcating, to some extent symbolically, space that is intended to be used for reflection and other learning activities, like experimentation, lecturing, and so on. The dimensions or shape of any space establish parameters and thereby set boundaries (how many people can participate and how they communicate) that affect the learning experience.

Another aspect of the dependency between learning and space pertains to how we store what we have learned. In the not-too-distant past, filing cabinets, bookshelves, and libraries were the principal repositories for paper documents. Unfortunately, as the size of any repository or information space expands, access to the knowledge stored therein is often jeopardized.

Computers, new information and communication technologies, and new ideas about how people work together have created ways to circumvent some of the limitations of space, affecting how people can learn together and how they store and retrieve what they have learned. For example, in the past formal training activities were constrained by the need to colocate training participants. Now "computer-supported learning" has led to training programs that are located on desktop computers or interactive computer discs.

While job aids, such as reference manuals and checklists, have historically been little more than crib sheets, now extensive knowledge about work tasks and problem solutions can be available at any time via computers and computer programs. Entire companies (and some might claim entire industries) have been created to help organizations with knowledge management, including search and retrieval via the Internet and the World Wide Web. Whether on their own or connected by networks, computers have exponentially expanded the space available to store information and have provided innovative methods (via computer software) to access and show data in presentational form. Customized computer programs can store all kinds of knowledge that contribute to learning. They may also function as learning feedback loops, with software used to track customer complaints, errors, and problems or to monitor work production and alter inputs or processes to improve quality.

Beyond the expansion of space to store explicit knowledge and the capability to make it more widely accessible, computers and new forms of telecommunication have also produced new ways for people to interact in order to create knowledge or learn from one another.

"No need to pack; just click": so reads the marketing literature for one company's software program that allows organizations to "train anywhere." (The same marketing brochure goes on to state that "traditional teaching methods are no longer sufficient. You need to break the barriers of time and location to allow you to improve the capabilities of everyone in your organization. . . . Now you can train anyone, anywhere, anytime. On-line or off-line.")

Such new technologies have produced new terminology, including e-learning (learning supported through electronic means), tele-learning (sharing knowledge and learning through voice transmission), and distance learning. The possibility now exists to combine voice and video transmissions (teleconferencing), to broadcast learning opportunities via satellite or the Internet, and to create work space on networked computers (the World Wide Web) that is accessible to any community, team, or group of learners (Beer, 2000). These capabilities mean that there are alternatives to training programs or courses and other learning events that have required the colocation of teachers, trainees, or fellow learners. Computer technology can now provide virtual learning spaces, campuses, and conferences that allow geographically separate individuals to participate in learning events either synchronously or asynchronously. Whether classified as groupware or on-line productivity tools, these technologies have redefined the meaning and limitations of space and time as dimensions to learning (Darrouzet et al., 1995).

An example of how new technologies can promote learning and spread it across space and time pertains to United Airlines Flight 232, which crashed in a cornfield outside Sioux City, Iowa, in 1989. As previously described in Chapter 4, transformational learning among the flight crew saved many passengers. In remembering the tenth-year anniversary of the incident, the local newspaper, the *Sioux City Journal,* established a Web Site on the Internet. The site (http://www.siouxcityjournal.com/Flight232) contains a wide range of information about the incident, including what the FAA learned from the crash, how the experience has led to better emergency planning, and what rescuers learned about their community and about coordination among various service agencies. The site is also a repository for the ongoing reflections of survivors and caregivers who live in various parts of the United States.

Progress in developing new mechanisms to circumvent the limitations of space and time as they affect learning has not been limited to computer-based or information technologies. OD experts have been developing methods and capabilities to reconfigure the use of space to support learning behaviors. "Open Space" (Owen, 1997), "Future Search" (Weisbord, 1995), and "Search Conferences" (Emery, 1996) are examples of innovative processes that use space to bring people together in new ways to generate knowledge, learning, and shared vision.

In Conclusion

While a learning time line can direct attention toward the sources of our learning, our horizon must also encompass new and emerging ways and possibilities to learn. Such developments have a way of altering characteristics such as space and time that have constrained previous modes of learning in our teams and organizations. Our learning horizon is simultaneously presented to us and created by us through our collective action and insight.

In this book, I have outlined an approach to team and organizational learning that acknowledges the ever changing stage upon which our actions take place. As we engage in practices that promote learning in our organizations today, we need be aware of the emerging methods we have at our disposal. In so doing, we learn about learning.

While recognizing our accomplishments to date and diagnosing our current capabilities, we must also keep our focus on shifting needs and possibilities. No one really knows what lies beyond our horizon; for this reason, learning and learning capability are critical yet evolving domains of emphasis for teams and organizations. Yet, it is the meaning and sense of ownership we bring to learning that make this capability effective and worthwhile. Ultimately, it is only through our own action (and adaptation) that such ownership and value are created.

Learning Practices: Lesson 10

What we need to learn and how we learn
change as we accrue experience and knowledge.
Time and space are constraints on our learning,
but new and evolving technologies create ways
to circumvent them. We should be aware of the
changing horizon of possibilities and needs.

References

Argyris, C. 1957. "The Individual and the Organization: Some Problems of Mutual Adjustment." *Administrative Science Quarterly* 2, 1–24.

Argyris, C. 1976. "Single-Loop and Double-Loop Models in Research on Decision-Making." *Administrative Science Quarterly* 21, 373–75.

Argyris, C., R. Putnam, and D. M. Smith. 1985. *Action Science.* San Francisco: Jossey-Bass.

Beckhard, R., and R. T. Harris. 1987. *Organizational Transitions: Managing Complex Change* (2nd ed.). Reading, MA: Addison-Wesley.

Beer, V. 2000. *The Web Learning Fieldbook: Using the World Wide Web to Build Workplace Learning Environments.* San Francisco: Jossey-Bass.

Botkin, J. 1999. *Smart Business: How Knowledge Communities Can Change Your Company.* New York: Free Press.

Brooking, A. 1996. *Intellectual Capital: Core Asset for the Third Millennium Enterprise.* Boston: International Thomson Business Press.

Brown, S. L., and K. M. Eisenhardt. 1998. *Competing on the Edge: Strategy as Structured Chaos.* Boston: Harvard Business School Press.

Bushe, G. R., and A. B. Shani. 1991. *Parallel Learning Structures: Increasing Innovation in Bureaucracies.* Reading, MA: Addison-Wesley.

Case, J. 1995. *Open-Book Management: The Coming Business Revolution.* New York: Harper Collins.

Center for Workforce Development. 1998. "The Teaching Firm: Where Productive Work and Learning Converge." Newton, MA: Education Development Center.

Collins, J. C., and J. I. Porras. 1994. *Built to Last: Successful Habits of Visionary Companies.* New York: Harper Collins.

Cyert, R. M., and J. G. March. 1963. *A Behavioral Theory of the Firm.* Upper Saddle River, NJ: Prentice Hall.

Darrouzet, C., et al. 1995. "Rethinking 'Distance' in Distance Learning." IRL Report 19.101. Menlo Park, CA: Institute For Research on Learning.

deGeus, A. P. 1988. "Planning as Learning." *Harvard Business Review,* March–April, 70–74.

Deming, W. E. 1982. *Out of the Crisis.* Cambridge, MA: MIT Technology Center of Advanced Engineering Study.

DiBella, A. J. 1990. "The Research Manager's Role in Encouraging Evaluation Use." *Evaluation Practice* 2, 115–19.

DiBella, A. J. 1992. *Culture and Planned Change in an International Organization: Building a Regional Structure in South America and Asia.* Ph.D. Dissertation, MIT Sloan School of Management.

DiBella, A. J. 1995. "Developing Learning Organizations: A Matter of Perspective." Paper presented at the Academy of Management meeting, Vancouver, Canada.

DiBella, A. J., and E. C. Nevis. 1998. *How Organizations Learn: An Integrated Strategy for Building Learning Capability.* San Francisco: Jossey-Bass.

DiBella, A. J., E. C. Nevis, and J. M. Gould. 1996. "Understanding Organizational Learning Capability." *Journal of Management Studies* 33, 361–79.

Edvinsson, L., and M. Malone. 1997. *Intellectual Capital: Realizing Your Company's True Value by Finding Its Hidden Roots.* New York: Harper Business.

Emery, M., and R. Purser. 1996. *The Search Conference: A Powerful Method for Planning Organizational Change and Community Action.* San Francisco: Jossey-Bass.

Garvin, D. A. 1993. "Building a Learning Organization." *Harvard Business Review,* July–August, 78–91.

Goffman, E. 1959. *The Presentation of Self in Everyday Life.* New York: Doubleday.

Hall, E. T. 1959. *The Silent Language.* New York: Doubleday.

Hall, E. T. 1966. *The Hidden Dimension.* New York: Doubleday.

Hamel, G., and C. K. Prahalad. 1994. *Competing for the Future.* Boston: Harvard Business School Press.

Hock, D. 1999. *Birth of the Chaordic Age.* San Francisco: Berrett-Koehler.

Hofstede, G. 1991. *Cultures and Organizations: Software of the Mind.* London: McGraw-Hill.

Honey, P., and A. Mumford. 1986. *The Manual of Learning Styles.* Maidenhead, England: Honey Publications.

Hudson, W. J. 1993. *Intellectual Capital: How to Build It, Enhance It, Use It.* New York: John Wiley.

Imai, M. 1989. *Kaizen: The Key to Japan's Competitive Success.* New York: McGraw-Hill.

Isaacs, W. 1999. *Dialogue and the Art of Thinking Together: A Pioneering Approach to Communicating in Business and Life.* New York: Doubleday.

Juran, J. M. 1992. *Juran on Quality by Design.* Free Press: New York.

Kaplan, R. S., and D. P. Norton. 1992 "The Balanced Scorecard—Measures That Drive Performance." *Harvard Business Review,* January–February, 71–79.

Kolb, D. A. 1974. "On Management and the Learning Process." In *Organizational Psychology: A Book of Readings* (2nd ed.), Kolb, Rubin, and McIntyre, eds., 27–41. Upper Saddle River, NJ: Prentice Hall.

Lave, J., and E. Wenger. 1991. *Situated Learning: Legitimate Peripheral Participation.* New York: Cambridge University Press.

Levitt, T. 1975. "Marketing Myopia." *Harvard Business Review,* September–October, 26–39.

Levitt, B., and J. G. March. 1988. "Organizational Learning." *Annual Review of Sociology* 14, 319–40.

March, J. C., and H. A. Simon. 1958. *Organizations.* New York: J. Wiley and Sons.

Markoff, J. 1993. "Where the Cubicle Is Dead." *New York Times,* 25 April 1993. Sec. #3, p. 7.

McGill, M. E., J. W. Slocum, and D. Lei. 1992. "Management Practices in Learning Organizations." *Organizational Dynamics* 21, summer, 5–17.

Michalski, J. 1997. "IRL: Learning Is Social." *Release 1.0*; EDventure Holdings, New York.

Mintzberg, H. 1994. *The Rise and Fall of Strategic Planning.* New York: Free Press.

Nevis, E. C., A. J. DiBella, and J. M. Gould. 1995. "Understanding Organizations as Learning Systems." *Sloan Management Review* 36, winter, 73–85.

Nystrom, P. C., and W. H. Starbuck. 1984. "To Avoid Organizational Crises, Unlearn." *Organizational Dynamics* 12, spring, 53–65.

Owen, H. 1997. *Expanding Our Now: The Story of Open Space Technology.* San Francisco: Berrett-Koehler.

Perrow, C. 1984. *Normal Accidents: Living with High-Risk Technologies.* New York: Basic Books.

Peters, T. J., and R. H. Waterman. 1982. *In Search of Excellence: Lessons from America's Best-Run Companies.* New York: Harper & Row.

Raelin, Joseph A. 1999. *Work-Based Learning: The New Frontier of Management Development.* Reading, MA: Addison-Wesley.

Ries, A., and J. Trout. 1981. *Positioning: The Battle for the Mind.* New York: McGraw-Hill.

Roberts, K., and G. Gargano. 1990. "Managing a High Reliability Organization: A Case for Interdependence." In *Managing Complexity in High Tech Organizations,* Von Glinow and Mohrman, eds., 146–59. New York: Oxford.

Robinson, A. G., and S. Stern. 1998. *Corporate Creativity.* San Francisco: Berrett-Koehler.

Roos, J. (ed.). 1998. *Intellectual Capital: Navigating in the New Business Landscape.* New York: New York University Press.

Rossi, P. H., H. E. Freeman, and M. W. Lipsey. 1999. *Evaluation: A Systematic Approach* (6th ed.). Thousand Oaks, CA: SAGE.

Roth, G., and A. Kleiner. 1998. "Developing Organizational Memory Through Learning Histories." *Organizational Dynamics* 27, autumn, 43–60.

Rouse, W. B. 1996. *Start Where You Are.* San Francisco: Jossey-Bass.

Schein, E. 1987. *Process Consultation Volume II: Lessons for Managers and Consultants.* Reading, MA: Addison-Wesley.

Schein, E. 1992. *Organizational Culture and Leadership* (2nd ed.). San Francisco: Jossey-Bass.

Schein, E. 1993. "How Can Organizations Learn Faster: The Challenge of Entering the Green Room." *Sloan Management Review* 34, winter, 85–90.

Schein, E. 1996. "The Three Cultures of Management: Implications for Organizational Learning." *Sloan Management Review* 38, 9–20.

Schein, E. 1999a. *Process Consultation Revisited: Building the Helping Relationship.* Reading, MA: Addison-Wesley.

Schein, E. 1999b. *The Corporate Culture Survival Guide.* San Francisco: Jossey-Bass.

Schon, D. 1984. *The Reflective Practitioner: Thinking in Action.* New York: Basic Books.

Senge, P. M. 1990. *The Fifth Discipline: The Art and Practice of the Learning Organization.* New York: Doubleday Currency.

Shepard, H. A. 1984. "Rules of Thumb for Change Agents." *OD Practitioner* 17, December, 2–7.

Shrivastava, P. 1983. "A Typology of Organizational Learning Systems." *Journal of Management Studies* 20, 7–28.

Snyder, W. M., and T. G. Cummings. 1992. "Organizational Learning Disabilities." Paper presented at the annual meeting of the Academy of Management, Las Vegas.

Srivastva, S., D. L. Cooperrider & Associates. 1999. *Appreciative Management and Leadership*: *The Power of Positive Thought and Action in Organizations* (revised ed.). Euclid, Ohio: Williams Custom Publishing.

Stata, R. 1989. "Organizational Learning: The Key to Management Innovation." *Sloan Management Review* 30, spring, 63–74.

Stewart, T. A. 1997. *Intellectual Capital: The New Wealth of Organizations.* New York: Doubleday.

Suchman, E. A. 1967. *Evaluative Research.* New York: Sage Foundation.

Van der Heijden, K. 1996. *Scenarios: The Art of Strategic Dialogue.* New York: John Wiley & Sons.

Watkins, K. E., and V. J. Marsick. 1993. *Sculpting the Learning Organization.* San Francisco: Jossey-Bass.

Weick, K. 1988. "Enacted Sensemaking in Crisis Situations." *Journal of Management Studies* 25, 305–17.

Weisbord, M., and S. Janoff. 1995. *Future Search: An Action Guide to Finding Common Ground in Organizations and Community.* San Francisco: Berrett-Koehler.

Wenger, E. 1998. *Communities of Practice: Learning, Meaning, and Identity.* Cambridge, England: Cambridge University Press.

Yow, V. R. 1994. *Recording Oral History: A Practical Guide for Social Scientists.* Thousand Oaks, CA: SAGE.

Zaltman, G., R. Duncan, and J. Holbeck. 1984. *Innovations and Organizations.* Malabar, FL: Krieger.

Index

OD Series

adult life cycle, interaction of work and family, and integration of individual and organizational goals through human resource planning and development are all thoroughly explored.

Work Redesign
J. Richard Hackman and Greg R. Oldham   1980 (0-201-02779-8)
This book is a comprehensive, clearly written study of work design as a strategy for personal and organizational change. Linking theory and practical technologies, it develops traditional and alternative approaches to work design that can benefit both individuals and organizations.

Pay and Organization Development
Edward E. Lawler   1981 (0-201-03990-7)
This book examines the important role that reward systems play in organization development efforts. By combining examples and specific recommendations with conceptual material, it organizes the various topics and puts them into a total systems perspective. Specific pay approaches such as gainsharing, skill-based pay, and flexible benefits are discussed, and their impact on productivity and the quality of work life is analyzed.

Organizational Transitions: Managing Complex Change, Second Edition
Richard Beckhard and Reuben T. Harris   1987 (0-201-10887-9)
This book discusses the choices involved in developing a management system appropriate to the "transition state." It also discusses commitment to change, organizational culture, and increasing and maintaining productivity, creativity, and innovation.

Stream Analysis: A Powerful Way to Diagnose and Manage Organizational Change
Jerry I. Porras   1987 (0-201-05693-3)
Drawing on a conceptual framework that helps the reader to better understand organizations, this book shows how to diagnose failings in organizational functioning and how to plan a comprehensive set of actions needed to change the organization into a more effective system.

Process Consultation, Volume II: Lessons for Managers and Consultants
Edgar H. Schein   1987 (0-201-06744-7)
This book shows the viability of the process consultation model for working with human systems. Like Schein's first volume on process consultation, the second volume focuses on the moment-to-moment behavior of the manager or consultant rather than the design of the OD program.

Managing Conflict: Interpersonal Dialogue and Third-Party Roles,
Second Edition
Richard E. Walton   1987 (0-201-08859-2)
This book shows how to implement a dialogue approach to conflict manage-
ment. It presents a framework for diagnosing recurring conflicts and suggests
several basic options for controlling or resolving them.

Power and Organization Development: Mobilizing Power to Implement
Change
Larry E. Greiner and Virginia E. Schein   1988 (0-201-12185-9)
This book forges an important collaborative approach between two opposing
and often contradictory approaches to management: OD practitioners who
espouse a "more humane" workplace without understanding the political
realities of getting things done, and practicing managers who feel comfort-
able with power but overlook the role of human potential in contributing to
positive results.

Designing Organizations for High Performance
David P. Hanna   1988 (0-201-12693-1)
This book is the first to give insight into the actual processes you can use to
translate organizational concepts into bottom-line improvements. Hanna's
"how-to" approach shows not only the successful methods of intervention,
but also the plans behind them and the corresponding results.

Process Consultation, Volume I, Second Edition: Its Role in Organization
Development, Second Edition
Edgar H. Schein   1988 (0-201-06736-6)
How can a situation be influenced in the workplace without the direct use of
power or formal authority? This book presents the core theoretical founda-
tions and basic prescriptions for effective management.

Change by Design
Robert R. Blake, Jane Srygley Mouton,   1989 (0-201-50748-X)
and Anne Adams McCanse
This book develops a systematic approach to organization development and
provides readers with rich illustrations of coherent planned change. The
book involves testing, examining, revising, and strengthening conceptual
foundations in order to create sharper corporate focus and increased pre-
dictability of successful organization development.

Managing in the New Team Environment: Skills, Tools, and Methods
Larry Hirschhorn   1991 (0-201-52503-8)
This text is designed to help manage the tensions and complexities that arise
for managers seeking to guide employees in a team environment. Based on
an interactive video course developed at IBM, the text takes managers step
by step through the process of building a team and authorizing it to act while
they learn to step back and delegate. Specific issues addressed include how to
give a team structure, how to facilitate its basic processes, and how to
acknowledge differences in relationships among team members and between
the manager and individual team members.

*Leading Business Teams: How Teams Can Use Technology and Group
Process Tools to Enhance Performance*
Robert Johansen, David Sibbett, Suzyn Benson,   1991 (0-201-52829-0)
Alexia Martin, Robert Mittman, and Paul Saffo
What technology or tools should organization development people or team
leaders have at their command, now and in the future? This text explores the
intersection of technology and business teams, a new and largely uncharted
area that goes by several labels, including "groupware"—a term that encom-
passes both electronic and nonelectronic tools for teams. This is the first
book of its kind from the field describing what works for business teams and
what does not.

The Conflict-Positive Organization: Stimulate Diversity and Create Unity
Dean Tjosvold   1991 (0-201-51485-0)
This book describes how managers and employees can use conflict to find
common ground, solve problems, and strengthen morale and relationships.
By showing how well-managed conflict invigorates and empowers teams and
organizations, the text demonstrates how conflict is vital for a company's
continuous improvement and increased competitive advantage.

Total Quality: A User's Guide for Implementation
Dan Ciampa   1992 (0-201-54992-1)
This is a book that directly addresses the challenge of how to make Total
Quality work in a practical, no-nonsense way. The companies that will dom-
inate markets in the future will be those that deliver high quality, competi-
tively priced products and service just when the customer wants them and in
a way that exceeds the customer's expectations. The vehicle by which these
companies move to that stage is Total Quality.

Organization Development: A Process of Learning and Changing, Second Edition
W. Warner Burke   1994 (0-201-50835-4)
This text provides a comprehensive overview of the field of organization development. Written for managers, executives, administrators, practitioners, and students, this book takes an in-depth look at organization development with particular emphasis on the importance of learning and change. The author not only describes the basic tenets of OD, but he also looks at OD as a change in an organization's culture. Frameworks and models like the Burke-Litwin model (Chapter 7), as well as numerous case examples, are used throughout the book to enhance the reader's understanding of the principles and practices involved in leading and managing organizational change.

Competing with Flexible Lateral Organizations, Second Edition
Jay R. Galbraith   1994 (0-201-50836-2)
This book focuses on creating competitive advantage by building a lateral capability, thereby enabling a firm to respond flexibly in an uncertain world. The book addresses international coordination and cross-business coordination as well as the usual cross-functional efforts. It is unique in covering both crossfunctional (lateral or horizontal) coordination, as well as international and corporate issues.

The Dynamics of Organizational Levels: A Change Framework for Managers and Consultants
Nicholas S. Rashford and David Coghlan   1994 (0-201-54323-0)
This book introduces the idea that, for successful change to occur, organizational interventions have to be coordinated across the major levels of issues that all organizations face. Individual level, team level, interunit level, and organizational level issues are identified and analyzed, and the kinds of intervention appropriate to each level are spelled out.

Team Building: Current Issues and New Alternatives, Third Edition
William G. Dyer   1995 (0-201-62882-1)
One of the major developments in the field of organization redesign has been the emergence of self-directed work teams. This book explains how teams are most successful when the team becomes part of the culture and structure or systems of the organization. It discusses the major new trends and emphasizes the degree of commitment that managers and members must bring to the team-building process. It is written for managers and human resource professionals who want to develop a more systematic program of team building in their organization or work unit.

Creating Labor-Management Partnerships

Warner P. Woodworth and Christopher B. Meek   1995 (0-201-58823-4)

This book begins with a call for changing the social and political barriers existing in unionized work settings and emphasizes the critical need for union-management cooperation in the present context of international competition. It demonstrates the shift from confrontational union-management relationships toward more effective and positive systems of collaboration. It is written for human resource management and industrial relations managers and staff, union officials, professional arbitrators and mediators, government officials, and professors and students involved in the study of organization development.

Organizational Learning II: Theory, Method, and Practice

Chris Argyris and Donald A. Schön   1996 (0-201-62983-6)

This text addresses how business firms, governments, non-governmental organizations, schools, health care systems, regions, and whole nations need to adapt to changing environments, draw lessons from past successes and failures, detect and correct the errors of the past, anticipate and respond to impending threats, conduct experiments, engage in continuing innovation, and build and realize images of a desirable future. There is a virtual consensus that we are all subject to a "learning imperative," and in the academy no less than in the world of practice, organizational learning has become an idea in good currency.

Integrated Strategic Change: How OD Builds Competitive Advantage

Christopher G. Worley, David E. Hitchin,   1996 (0-201-85777-4)
and Walter L. Ross

This book is about strategic change and how firms can improve their performance and effectiveness. Its unique contribution is in describing how organization development practitioners can assist in the effort. Strategic change is a type of organization change that realigns an organization's strategy, structure, and process within a given competitive context. It is substantive and systemic and therefore differs from traditional organization development that produces incremental improvements, addresses only one system at a time, or does not intend to increase firm-level performance.

Developing Network Organizations: Learning from Theory and Practice

Rupert F. Chisholm   1998 (0-201-87444-X)

The interorganizational network is rapidly emerging as a key type of organization, and the importance of the network is expected to increase throughout the 21st century. This text covers the process of developing these complex systems. The author uses in-depth description and analysis based on direct involvement with three diverse networks to identify critical aspects of the development process. He explains relevant concepts and appropriate methods and practices in the context of developing these three networks, and he also identifies ten key learnings derived from his direct involvement with the development process.

Diagnosing and Changing Organizational Culture
Kim S. Cameron and Robert E. Quinn   1999 (0-201-33871-8)
This book helps managers, change agents, and scholars to understand, diagnose, and facilitate the change of an organization's culture in order to enhance its effectiveness. The authors present three forms of assistance for readers: (1) validated instruments for diagnosing organizational culture and management competency, (2) a theoretical framework for understanding organizational culture, and (3) a systematic strategy and methodology for changing organizational culture and personal behavior. This text is a workbook in that readers can complete the instruments and plot their own culture profile in the book itself. They can also use the text as a resource for understanding and leading a culture change process.

Process Consultation Revisited: Building the Helping Relationship
Edgar H. Schein   1999 (0-201-34596-X)
The latest addition to Ed Schein's well-loved set of process consultation books, this new volume builds on the content of the two that precede it while expanding to explore the critical area of the helping relationship. *Process Consultation Revisited* focuses on the interaction between consultant and client, explaining how to achieve the healthy helping relationship so essential to effective consultation. Whether the advisor is an OD consultant, therapist, social worker, manager, parent, or friend, the dynamics between advisor and advisee can be difficult to understand and manage. Drawing on over 40 years of experience as a consultant, Schein creates a general theory and methodology of helping that will enable a diverse group of readers to navigate the helping process successfully.

Work-Based Learning: The New Frontier of Management Development
Joseph A. Raelin   2000 (0-201-43388-5)
This timely book introduces a unique but very practical approach to work-based learning. Recognizing the limits of a pure classroom model, the book acknowledges the workplace as the "new frontier," and demonstrates how work-based learning is acquired in the midst of practice but expressly intersects knowledge with experience. Grounded in theory but incredibly practical with frequent use of realistic examples.